^{101} Uses *for* This Book

101
Uses *for*
This
Book

Paul Grescoe

ILLUSTRATIONS BY BRUCE ROBERTS

RAINCOAST BOOKS
Vancouver

First published in 1996 by
Raincoast Book Distribution Ltd.
8680 Cambie Street
Vancouver, B.C.
v6p 6m9
(604) 323-7100

1 3 5 7 9 10 8 6 4 2

CANADIAN CATALOGUING IN PUBLICATION DATA

Grescoe, Paul, 1939-
101 uses for this book

ISBN 1-55192-009-3

1. Canadian wit and humor (English).* 2. Books – Humor. 3. Canadian wit
and humor, Pictorial. 4. Books – Caricatures and cartoons.
I. Roberts, Bruce, 1946- II. Title. III. Title: One
hundred and one uses for this book.

PS8563.R37073 1996   C818'.5402   C95-910868-8
PR9199.3.G73073 1996

Designed by Dean Allen
Project Editor: Michael Carroll
Copy Editor: Rachelle Kanefsky
Cover Illustration by Bruce Roberts

Printed and bound in Canada

ACKNOWLEDGMENTS

I must acknowledge the contribution of Canadian artist Iain Baxter, who cofounded the ever-inventive N.E. Thing Co. three decades ago, and whose brainstorming with me so many years ago on the creative uses of a book proved an inspiration for this project. Many thanks to my son, Taras, and his wife, Gwénaëlle, my daughter, Lara, and my wife, Audrey, who collectively came up with so many of the best and wittiest uses chronicled in these pages (and, because of Audrey, I finally know how to make a Shelleyesque paper boat). And a round of applause to the infinitely patient librarians of the Vancouver Public Library and the University of British Columbia, who helped direct me on my whimsical quest.

INTRODUCTION

I have sought for happiness everywhere, but I have found it nowhere except in a little corner with a little book.

– Thomas à Kempis, 15th-century
German monk and author

That was then. This is now. Hypermedia, the Information Highway, the Bit Bang, Virtual Reality, all the vaunted interactivity of cyberspace and media technology – who needs or wants the traditional bound volume of printed words and pictures?

Is the book dead?

Any way you read it: No.

Books, the Canadian media guru Marshall McLuhan declared in the early 1960s, are too slow and are therefore redundant. Three decades along, the British Library reports that, although the amount of information it stores digitally is increasing every year, the "amount of paper that is stored annually will not diminish."

For very good reasons. The uses of the book number endlessly more than the 101 I have chronicled in these pages. What we are celebrating here is the Book as Abiding Artifact: a tangible object, portable and convenient to use, entertaining and inspirational and educational, which by its very palpability and practicality will endure in an age of computers and the Internet.

Try pressing flowers or collecting autographs with a computer. Or swatting flies or dogs' bottoms with it. Go ahead: take a PC into the tub to read from, without worrying about water damage; or deftly scroll to the next page of *Neuromancer* on your laptop while dangling from a strap on the subway; or happily balance a PowerBook on your knees as you sit on the john devouring a Danielle Steel on CD-ROM. For that matter, try reading an entire novel anywhere, comfortably, on the best of active-matrix color screens. Nor would I

I

advise using your $2,000 Mac as a posture improver, a booby trap, or an eyeshade on the beach – all peripheral yet pragmatic and traditional uses for a book, documented between the covers of this one.

A book, the scoffers say, is merely ink that lies inertly, passively on paper. Yet is there anything more truly interactive than the dialogue between a good book and its reader? Or more passive than the connection between computers and language? Oh, they talk of being able to rewrite someone else's hypertext novel on screen, become a coauthor, pursue other ideas or pathways of the plot that even the writer hadn't conceived. But of course to surrender ourselves to a work of fiction – rather than collaborating to reshape it – is to listen to another human's voice and mind, to wallow in the beauty of the words or the technique behind the style, and to park our own prejudices at least temporarily.

When it comes to reading for pleasure or the mind expansion of literature, computers just don't hack it. Nicholas Negroponte is head of the Massachusetts Institute of Technology's Media Lab and author of *Being Digital*, in which he rhapsodizes about information technology. Still, even he allows that "the written word sparks images and evokes metaphors" while electronic media "leave very little to the imagination."

For reference works, yes, they can be wonderful. For a school kid to tap into *Encyclopaedia Britannica* and find all the allusions to Fig Newtons in one fell keypunch. Or for a master's student in literature to plug into the database that a Virginia company has compiled on CD-ROM of all the works of 1,350 poets from the years 600 to 1900. It's possible, too, that the Internet user can make the same serendipitous discoveries in cyberspace that the reader does while browsing in libraries or bookshops.

Yet compared to the unedited, often anonymous ephemera on the Internet, the book may be the most trustworthy information-provider we have. The traditional book undergoes a process of selection and editing that, at its best, assures some credibility. A writer has signed his or her name to it and submitted the ideas and information to the scrutiny of an editor and a publisher who have questioned and criticized and amended and clarified. "The information highway is being sold to us as delivering information, but what it's really delivering is data," says Clifford Stoll, author of *Silicon Snake Oil: Second Thoughts on the Information Highway*, and once a defender of the Internet. "Unlike data," he said in a recent interview, "information has utility, timeliness, accuracy, a pedigree. Information, I can trust."

Nor is the computer the only hypothetical competitor to the book. Television and videos tell stories and communicate information, but – despite the old adage – I have yet to see a picture worth a thousand words (101, perhaps). In the words of editor and author Norman Cousins, "no visual image is as vivid as the image created by the mind in response to words." Film is swell for action but not introspection; interior monologues and other adventures of the mind do not make it on the screen.

A sign once posted in the University of Wisconsin library bore this unattributed message:

> Books are quiet. They do not dissolve into wavy lines or snowstorm effects. They do not pause to deliver commercials. They are three-dimensional, having length, breadth, and depth. They are convenient to handle and completely portable.

Audiotapes, too, have tried to substitute for the printed volume. But the time it takes for actors to read a whole book is daunting. The personal interpretation they bring to an author's words makes the listener a passive audience – and how many times would you have to replay a reading of Northrop Frye's critique of the Bible, *The Great Code*, before cracking its meaning?

Before tapes, TV, and the computer came along, the radio and the telephone were supposed to spell doom for book reading. What the Jeremiahs have seldom acknowledged, however, is the pure utility, the sheer expediency of the package we call a book. A book is discreet enough to go places where Walkmans and tape recorders, computers and cellular phones are not welcome. Restaurants, for

3

instance. And like me, the American film historian and biographer Kenneth Turan enjoys nothing more than dining out with a book: "A book does not make bad jokes, drink too much, or eat more than you can afford to pay for."

As well as being cheap dates, books can be gorgeous. Michael Joyce, an English professor at Vassar College and creator of *Afternoon*, a hypertext novel for the computer, insists we are moving toward many more such books. Yet he has admitted that "regular books are beautiful, sustaining objects that have their own sensuality that I hope will never disappear."

Let us hope. In a society that was supposed to be turning paperless, book sales continue to climb. The book and its ancestors have endured for 2,000 years. We still have a copy of the oldest complete printed book known, the Chinese *Diamond Sutra*, a Buddhist work written in Sanskrit, dated 868.

And as *101 Uses for This Book* attempts to demonstrate, tongue only partly in cheek, the book remains alive and, well, find a little corner, and see for yourself.

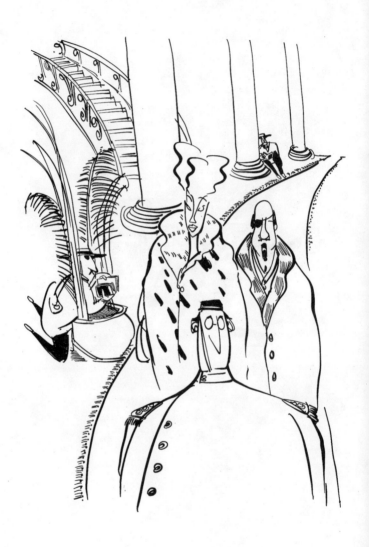

1 · CODE BOOK

HITLER TO ATTACK RUSSIA. The warning, translated from an elaborate number code into English, arrived in Moscow in the spring of 1941. The unbelievable message was transmitted at least a week before Germany's invasion of its uneasy ally. The accurate informant was the greatest spy of World War II: Rudolf Roessler, or Lucy, nicknamed for Lucerne, Switzerland, the base of operations for the war's most successful spy operation. The coding device was a bulky book of statistics – both transmitter and receiver had a copy at hand to decipher the radioed message.

But the Lucy ring soon began using more portable books, such as pocket-sized volumes of Shakespeare, with the letters of the alphabet translated into figures, in reverse order from 26 to one. Throughout the war Lucy's by-the-book intelligence reports kept Russia a crucial step ahead of Germany and helped stop the enemy in its tracks at the pivotal Battle of Stalingrad.

Books have been a popular and practical way of delivering coded information, in fact and fiction. In *The Key to Rebecca* thriller writer Ken Follett has his German master spy use Daphne du Maurier's darkly romantic novel as a code book. His system sounds complicated but is devilishly simple. To select the page of the book to use in creating the cipher, Alex Wolff would add the last two digits of the year – '42, say – to the number of the day of the month. Then if it happened to be May, the fifth month, he discounted every fifth letter on the page. Wishing to say HAVE ARRIVED, he would begin at the top of the page and might find that, not counting the fifth letter, *H* was the 10th letter on the first line. *H* then became represented by the 10th letter of the alphabet, *J*. If *A* was the third letter following the *H*, it would be represented by the third letter of the alphabet, *C*. And so on, in a cipher that was breakable only if the interceptor knew both the book in question and the rudimentary key to cracking the code.

A more recent example of a book code appears in *The Egyptian Jukebox* by Nick Bantock, creator of the bestselling *Griffin & Sabine* trilogy. The mysterious and fancifully designed *Jukebox* uses an uncomplicated cryptogram – secret writing – to point at words that spell out messages to help solve the book's puzzles. By using the variation of this cipher that follows, you can unveil the answer that lies within the very lines and words of the classic riddle posed in Use No. 75 (on page 112) of this book:

Ln 5, wd 6	Ln 13, wd 2	Ln 1, wd 4
Ln 6, wd 12	Ln 15, wd 9	Ln 13, wd 5
Ln 4, wd 8	Ln 15, wd 2	Ln 16, wd 4
Ln 8, wd 12	Ln 7, wd 12	Ln 12, wd 5
Ln 8, wd 5	Ln 5, wd 11	Ln 9, wd 3
	Ln 11, wd 10	

2 · FLOWER PRESS

A good book can press you – to finish it and reap the richness preserved within its pages. But almost any book can *be* a press – to hold the richness of the favorite flowers you reap in field and garden and to preserve them within its pages.

Flower-pressing in books is an old custom. In his 14th-century work, *The Philobiblon*, Richard de Bury of England speaks of the sloppy scholar who mistreats his manuscripts: "He goes out in the rain, and now flowers make their appearance upon our soil. Then the scholar we are describing, the neglect rather than the inspector of books, stuffs his volume with firstling violets, roses, and quadrifoils." Librarians have long found flowers – as well as leaves and four-leaf clovers, even feathers and butterflies – in volumes returned following picnics and bookish jaunts in the countryside.

This book, compact in size and with relatively absorbent pages, is ideal as a temporary press to hold any rosebuds or lobelia ye gather as ye may. It's a little handier to tote than the one-volume *Columbia Encyclopedia*, for instance. But once back home, you may want to employ books with the heft of that 2,400-page reference work. Place your floral or herbal specimens carefully between folded sheets of newspaper or the pages of a large telephone book (in layers about a quarter-inch thickness apart). Then use several heavy tomes – heavy in weight, not necessarily thought – to press the plants for about two months until they're as thin as the paper that dried them into delicate keepsakes of summer.

3 · CONTRACEPTIVE

Since 1993 England's *Literary Review* has offered the Grand Booby Prize for Bad Sex in Fiction. The judges, led by Auberon Waugh, take pains to point out that the prize is truly a Fiction Improvement Award given to draw attention to a bad or unsuccessful description of sex – "it should be humorless and redundant to the story."

The first year's winner was from Melvyn Bragg's *A Time to Dance* (Hodder and Stoughton), which included this passage:

> We twisted and tugged desperately at each other's buttons and zips, wanting to pause, wanting to go on, wanting to enjoy anticipation, wanting to be satiated. Most often you wore no bra and those wonderful breasts rode into my cupped hands and my mouth so firmly, so tenderly that there was a thud in my heart – to be so lucky. Your hands would rush nervously up and down my back, down my flanks as we tried to kiss, talk, embrace, undress and feel each other all in the same instant. Frantically we would separate and throw off clothes so fiercely that we often found rips and tears in them later. We would stand back and look at each other. . . . I still wonder how I could keep my sperm under control for so long. I became rather proud of it.

The most recent winner was Philip Hook's *The Stonebreakers* (also from Hodder and Stoughton). A sampling:

> As he eased the jacket from her shoulders, his tongue was already working against her teeth. Her tee shirt rode up and he felt her naked skin. Their jaws ground in a feverish mutual mastication. Saliva and sweat. Sweat and saliva. . . .
>
> Soon they were no longer bodies on a bed. They became some mad mobile sculpture manipulated this way and that in the throes of its own creation; two forms in search of positions of perfect linkage.

5 · COLORING BOOK

"Can you remember the pleasure you had as a child at the pure, white, unspoiled pages of a new coloring book?" asks Dr. Joseph Gold, an English professor at Ontario's University of Waterloo and a marriage and family therapist, in *Read for Your Life*. "It's like a field of snow waiting for your angel. The outlines are there, not oppressive, rather an opportunity. Then there is the power lying in wait in a good new sharp set of crayons or pencils – all the choices, all the bright promise and all yours to control. This heady power of creativity can be an intense pleasure to children."

Anna Lou Ashby, Andrew W. Mellon Curator of New York's Pierpoint Morgan Library, says that in England "a certain number of books created with woodcuts were issued with handcoloring or without, before the Victorian period [pre-1837], and occasionally I have seen copies of the 'without' that have been colored by their owners. As late as 1885 Ruskin issued an edition of *Dame Wiggins of Lee* [a children's book generally ascribed to Richard Scrafton Sharpe and a Mrs. Pearson] without color so that children could color it themselves, if they wished."

The illustrations in coloring books are generally crude, but a few books have approached the level of art. In the 1920s and 1930s French illustrator Françoise Seignobosc created lighthearted, peasantlike – and critically praised – line drawings for such titles as *Fanchette and Jeannot* and *The Little Green Cart*. In 1970 the renowned American illustrator Maurice Sendak made a coloring book version of his classic children's story, *In the Night Kitchen*, which knee-jerk critics castigated, one of them comparing it to "a sow's ear."

Coloring books have long had bad press; most educators reviled them for inhibiting a child's free creative development. More recently revisionists like Joseph Gold have argued that such books are a useful teaching tool that can give kids a deeper understanding and appreciation of art, not to mention better mental health. "Could it be," asks Irvin L. King of the University of Hawaii in the journal *Studies in Art Education*, "that one of the reasons coloring books are so popular is that they do provide emotional relief for children?"

And for adults, too? In *Eight Steps to a Healthy Heart* medical journalist Robert E. Kowalski seriously suggests that a potential or actual heart attack victim buy a coloring book and a box of crayons to relieve stress. You'd be surprised at how soothing coloring can be, he says, especially if you get goofy and color the hair green and the sky purple.

6 · MUSCLE BUILDER

(*Onetime Use Only*)

If you're not a strongman, stage magicians have a secret to help you tear a book in half: bake it in the oven at a low heat (watch to make sure it doesn't catch fire), cool to room temperature, and let it rip.

Leo Tolstoy, the author of *War and Peace*, was no strongman, but he did use books to develop his moral fiber and, incidentally, his muscles. As a boy, he believed that "a man accustomed to endure sufferings cannot be unhappy – and to inure myself to hardship, regardless of the severe pain I felt, I used to hold Tatischev's dictionaries out at arm's length for five minutes at a time. . . ."

7 · MORALIZER

The Babees Boke or a Lytyl Reporte of How Young People Should Behave – written around 1475 – proferred advice that members of the Moral Majority might promulgate today.

It urged youngsters to "look at people who speak to them and listen until they have finished without letting their eyes wander about the house. Until they are told to sit down, they are to stand quietly, are not to turn their backs to anyone nor interfere when their lord or lady is talking about the household. Especially are young people cautioned about their table manners: they are not to lean on the table, or fill their mouths too full or eat with their knives. . . ."

Lacking any light alternatives, kids in the 15th through 18th centuries embraced adult books, such as Daniel Defoe's thrilling *Robinson Crusoe* and Jonathan Swift's satirical *Gulliver's Travels*. It wasn't until author and publisher John Newbery came on the scene in mid-1700s England that sheer entertainment was first wed to education. Newbery, whose name is now commemorated in an annual North American children's book prize, published small flowered and gilded books, among them *The History of Little Goody Two-Shoes*. (That may have been the first kids' book to contain advertising. Goody Two-Shoes' father was "seized with a violent fever in a place where Dr. James' Powder was not to be had" – the powder being a patent medicine to which Newbery had bought the rights.) And nearly a century later another English author, Catherine Sinclair, wrote a trailblazing book, *Holiday House*, that celebrated the high spirits and naughtiness of youth. Children, she said, should be like "wild horses on the prairies, rather than like well-broken hacks on the road."

(For the Cowardly)

I was here, wait for me.
– Godot

– University of California at Berkeley

BIG BOOZE-UP IN THE STACKS NEXT TUESDAY.
EVERYONE WELCOME.

Please specify which Tuesday.
I've been coming every Tuesday for six weeks now.

– Women's washroom, University of Toronto

Moby Dick was a honkie

– Library staff lounge, Fort Belvoir, Virginia

Damn your writing,
Mind your shiting.

– Boghouse, Pancras-Wells,
England, cited in 1731

WHAT CANADA NEEDS NOW IS A NORTHROP FRYE COLORING BOOK

– Toronto, home of the late distinguished literary critic

NORMAN MAILER IS THE MASTER OF THE SINGLE ENTENDRE

– Ladies' room, Limelight Restaurant, New York City

Shakespeare eats Bacon. IT CAN'T BE DONNE

– Lion's Head Pub, New York City

THE PEN IS, MIGHTIER THAN THE SWORD

– Amendment to New York literacy poster, circa 1960

The first picture book published for children was *Kunst und Lehrbüchlein* of 1580, a book of art and instruction whose woodcuts included the first printed illustration of a child holding a doll. The first comic book was Jemmy Catnach's *Life in London; Or, The Sprees of Tom, Jerry, and Logick* of 1822. But the first kids' book with pictures that moved was a Better Little Book of 1940, *Big Chief Wahoo and the Magic Lamp*. (In *The Magic Magic Book*, the Whitney Museum of American Art's amazing $1,200 volume about magicians' books, Ricky Jay makes note of early "flick books," which gave the illusion of animation through the riffling of pages of sequential illustrations. Most likely designed with adults in mind, flick books were patented in England and Europe in 1868 and 1882; one with photographs was published in Berlin in 1892.)

Whitman Publishing Company of Racine, Wisconsin, had begun releasing Big Little Books in 1932. Five-by-five-inch volumes, they usually had 432 pages alternating between the story and black-and-white illustrations of characters from radio, comic strips, and movies. It was film cartoons that inspired Whitman's series of flip-it books – under the new name, Better Little Books – which had a sequence of small animated drawings in the upper right corner of each right-hand page (the company's All Pictures Comics books later had a second flip-it feature on the left-hand page). Under the heading "See 'em Move," the back covers often carried the simple instructions: "HOW IT'S DONE: Just flip the pages with your thumb."

The most elegant flip-it was conceived for *The Great Canadian Sonnet*, a book published in 1974, with a story by Canadian novelist David McFadden and the 60 animated illustrations created by one of Canada's finest artists, Greg Curnoe.

Wanna try, for old time's sake, or for the first time? Flip the corners of this book, front to back, for an animation surprise.

10 · CACHE

The 1994 film *The Shawshank Redemption*, based on a short story by Stephen King, is a bit of a paean to books. The most beloved character, a lifetime convict played by James Whitmore, runs the prison library, delivering books cell to cell. But the most pointed tribute to the power of the Word is the hiding place that the Tim Robbins character chooses to secrete a rock hammer: the hollowed-out pages of a Bible. Before escaping through the tunnel he's carved, the hero leaves the Bible in the safe of the rabidly religious warden, with the message: "You were right. Salvation lay within." And naturally, when the warden opens up the Old Testament to discover the cache for the hammer, the chapter title is Exodus.

Not so farfetched a story, given the reality of what happened in Colditz, the castle stronghold where the Nazis imprisoned the most troublesome Allied officers during World War II. In early 1942 a German censor who'd worked in publishing observed that some covers of hardback books sent to prisoners from Portugal were fatter than normal. For good reason. In these covers he found German currency, maps of escape routes, compasses, even hacksaw blades. The prison commandant immediately asked the Allied librarian for all the Portuguese books then out on loan. When they came back that afternoon, the books had the same plump covers but all the contraband had been removed and the endpapers reglued. From then on the prisoners could receive only paperbacks.

11 · TV CRITIC

Appropriately enough, the first book about TV – *Television*, by Alfred Dinsdale – had a frontispiece portrait of one of the tube's creators, the Scottish inventor John Logie Baird. It was published in 1926, the very year Baird first demonstrated true TV with a televisor that was partly mechanical, partly electronic. Two years later he televised across the Atlantic and showed off the first color TV.

In recent decades books about television, a competing medium, have been less celebrations of the technology than censure of its content. A sampling:

> *Mission Impossible* is glop from the shlock-hopper.
>
> > – Clive James of England's *The Observer*
> > in *Visions Before Midnight*.

> Both *Sesame Street* and *The Electric Company* not only teach an unabashedly linear approach to literacy and education but, in addition, do so within a context of propounding what are generally called white middle-class values – perhaps one might call them *higher* white middle-class values.
>
> > – Michael J. Arlen, *The View from
> > Highway 1: Essays on Television*.

> [Bob] Hoskins…was nasty, brutish, and short.…Making Iago a giggling psychopath reduces the tragedy to victimisation.
>
> > – Russell Davies of the London *Times*,
> > collected in *Shakespeare on Television*.

We call them Twinkies. You've seen them on television acting the news, modelling and fracturing the news while you wonder whether they've read the news – or if they've blow-dried their brains, too.

> – Linda Ellerbee, TV journalist, *And So It Goes*.

Scene for scene this heavily socially conscious epic [the series *Roots*] was not too compelling, but America needed it as a kind of expiation….

> – Leslie Haliwell, *Haliwell's Teleguide*.

Television suppresses and replaces creative human imagery, encourages mass passivity, and trains people to accept authority. It is an instrument of transmutation, turning people into their TV images.

> – Jerry Mander, *Four Arguments for the Elimination of Television*.

12 · DIARY OF A WEEKEND

(Otherwise Lost)

J. M. Barrie, the author of *Peter Pan*, said that the "life of every man is a diary in which he means to write one story, and writes another; and his humblest hour is when he compares the volume as it is with what he vowed to make it." If you haven't already begun a diary, this book offers you the perfect launch pad: a page to record your next weekend, when you might be relaxed enough to chronicle the events and your thoughts and feelings. And if you need further motivation, remember Colonel Ernest Loftus of Zimbabwe who started his diary at age 12 and wrote in it every day until his death in 1987 at 103.

SATURDAY

SUNDAY

23

13 · APHRODISIAC

There are about 1,800 romance novels published each year in North America – a half-billion-dollar business that produces more than 48 percent of all mass-market paperbacks bought on the continent. No longer are they about clinging British virgins who get to kiss the aloof but sensitive hero on the last page. The heroines are independent and demanding, and the sex they indulge in is often as unrestrained, if not as outright raunchy, as the readers' letters in *Penthouse Forum*. Inspired by this renaissance of romantic literature, we offer you a provocative passage in authentic romance writer's prose – while leaving significant blanks that you can fill in anew each time you read it:

> Shaun could not avert his hungry gaze from her —, so ineffectively concealed by the wet — that clung to her body like a —. Lying langorously on the —, looking at him over one bare alabaster shoulder, Cassie watched his — eyes rove over the fullness of her —, still damp and — in anticipation. Her upthrusting — must seem — to him, she thought, the dusky pink — waiting only for his — to make her shudder with desire. The scent of her — mingled with the — smell of the —. Remembering the — she had concealed from him until this moment, she placed it in her —. Now his — moved hotly over her — while his hands roamed her — , caressing, then kneading them in a fierce grip.
>
> With the barest hint of a smile, he said, "Cassandra Rhodes, it's time. We're going to — — and —."
>
> She gasped, realizing he would believe she was shocked, not —. "No, my love," she replied eagerly, insistently, "not until you — and — me first."

How to turn this book (or any unwanted paperback book of this size) into a permanent recipe card holder in four easy steps:

1. Placing book on solid surface, open it at exact center.

2. Fold left-hand page in half, into center; then fold right-hand page in half, into center. Crease each fold sharply with a finger.

3. Fold the second page on the left in half, into the center, behind the first fold. Continue folding each page in half, alternately, in this way until all the pages, and the front and back covers, are folded.

4. For added strength, glue cardboard backing to the folded cover.

Now lay the book on its cover. The folds form a fan to hold recipe cards for handy reference as you work in the kitchen. (A larger folded paperback, standing on end, will make an effective doorstop.)

Witch-hunting had become a popular sport in England during the late 16th century. So much so that a retired justice of the peace in Kent felt compelled to publish a treatise dispelling any notion that magicians and other tricksters required Satan's assistance. In 1584 Reginald Scot's *The Discoverie of Witchcraft* became what's believed to be the first book in English to deal with conjuring, from simple card tricks to a bodiless-head illusion. This pioneering work on magic was still in print four centuries later.

Books are a common magician's prop. The American illusionist Joseph Dunninger once explained an easy yet effective mind-reading stunt called the Book Miracle. While the magician leaves the room, a member of the audience opens a large book at any page, focuses on the first few sentences, and then closes the book. Returning, the performer reopens the book at the same page and reads the correct passage aloud.

The secret: the magician has glued a piece of hair about six inches long to the edge of the book's front cover. When the volume is opened, the hair automatically drops on to the chosen pages, where it remains when the book is closed – as a bookmark supposedly visible only to the mind reader.

A book known as *A Void* had a lot of publicity in U.S. journals following its 1994 publication in translation. Admiring critics say it's a "wildly amusing" smorgasbord of mind pranks, conundrums, and laws that its author turns topsy-turvy just to affirm actuality. And if you think this paragraph is awkward and wordy in construction, try writing a full book without using the fifth – and most common – symbol in our ABCs.

For a start, you can never write the most common word in English: *the*.

A Void was originally written in French, then translated into English without once using the letter *E*. Oddly the author's name itself bulges with the vowel: Georges Perec. But he was not the first to attempt such an E-viction. In 1939 Ernest Vincent Wright published *Gadsby*, a 50,000-word book that he wrote by tying a string to the E key on his typewriter and tapping patiently away until he found words and sentences that worked without it. A sample to inspire you, in case you want to write your own E-radicating book:

> And so, coming to Broadway, a booming brass drum and sounds of singing told of a small Salvation Army unit carrying on amidst Broadway's night shopping crowds. Gadsby, walking toward that group, saw a young girl, back toward him, just finishing a long soulful oration, saying, "…and I can say this to you, for I know what I am talking about; for I was brought up *in a pool of liquor!*"

There have been other letterless books. The 18th-century German poet Gottlob Burmann composed 20,000 words of poetry without the letter *R*. And in his 1862 work, *The Book-Hunter*, British bibliophile John Hill Burton tells of the poor unidentified French author "who, in a new edition of his works, desired to alter the old-fashioned spelling of the imperfect tense from 'o' to 'a.'" Unfortunately his printer went overboard and excluded *O* from the book entirely. "Even the sacred name of Napoleon was irreverently printed Napalean," Burton reports, "and the Revolution was the Revalutian."

Taking a favorite book or two along as you go on life's final journey has a long tradition. The ancient Egyptians and Romans were wont to do this; many distinguished mummies have been found with one rolled manuscript, but usually with not more than two rolls at a time. Papyrus that had been used to make papier-mâché cases for mummies – which eventually came to rest at the Sorbonne in Paris – was found in the early 1960s to contain most of a lost play, *Sikyonios*, written by Menander, the influential Greek poet and playwright, in about 300 B.C. In 687 the Celtic bishop St. Cuthbert was buried in a wooden coffin with a small Gospel of St. John beneath his head. When monks in Durham, England, opened the casket in 1104, they found both the book and the body remarkably preserved. Legend has it that the beautifully bound Gospel began performing miracles. It now rests in a glass case on loan to the British Library.

"From time immemorial humanity has craved the boon of carrying to the grave some book particularly loved in life," the 19th-century American book collector Eugene Field writes in *Love Affairs of a Bibliomaniac*. He should talk: before his death he compiled a list of two dozen books to be interred with him. As he explained in a little poem:

> *Then when the crack*
> *Of doom rolls back*
> *The marble and the earth that hide me,*
> *I'll smuggle home*
> *Each precious tome*
> *Without a fear a wife shall chide me.*

18 · MAUSOLEUM

(A Repository for Deservedly Dead Words)

Adscititious (adjective): Counterfeit, false; supplementary (18th century); from the Latin *ad* (to) + *sciscere* (to acknowledge), if that helps. "Sir, were you trying to pass an adscititious 50-dollar bill?"

Blind man's holiday (noun): Night, darkness (late 16th century; in late 19th to 20th century, Standard English).

Conjobble (verb): To settle, arrange; to chat (late 17th century). "Oh, nothing, we're just conjobbling."

Deadly nevergreen (noun): The gallows (late 18th, early 19th centuries, when hanging was still a fun public spectacle in England).

Firkytoodle (verb): To engage in intimate physical affection, as a prelude to sexual intercourse (17th to 19th century).

Lopadotemachoselachogaleokranioleipsanodrimhypotrimmatosilphioparaomelitokatakechymenokichlepikossyphophattoperisteralktryonoptekephalliokigklopeleiolagoiosiraiobaphetraganopterygon (noun): A stew of 17 sweet and acid ingredients, among them honey, vinegar, brains, mullet, and ouzo (circa 392 B.C.); coined by Aristophanes in his satire *The Ecclesiazusea* or *The Women in Politics*. The longest (and maybe the dumbest) word in literary history.

Mumble-sparrow (noun): A sport at fairs and wakes in which a handicapped man bites off the head of a handicapped cock sparrow (late 18th to early 19th century).

Spado (noun): A eunuch (15th century); from the Greek *spadon*; in 1646 Sir Thomas Browne writes in *Vulgar Errors*: "They live longest in every kinde that exercise it not at all, and this is true not only in eunuches by nature, but in spadoes by art!" Oh, yeah.

Thorough-go-nimble (noun): Diarrhea (late 17th century); also, lousy beer.

Trump (noun): A good chap (early 19th century; usage obsolete in 20th century – especially in reference to Donald Trump); also, the breaking of wind (mid-19th century).

19 · VICE

An anonymous pamphleteer in the England of 1874 was forced to use the very Devil's Tool he was condemning when he wrote in *The Vice of Reading*: "Reading is a stumbling block, a cloak thrown over ignorance, a softening, demoralising, relaxing practice, which, if persisted in, will end by enfeebling the minds of men and women, making flabby the fibre of their bodies, and undermining the vigour of nations."

As if that isn't enough, some Archfiends of Publishing have married the sin of reading to other wickedness. In the early days of this century a major tobacco company included a miniature volume of Shakespeare in every pack of cigarettes. And in 1916 Harry Scherman had the idea of inserting copies of the Little Leather Library of Shakespearean plays in boxes of Whitman's candy. The promotion was successful: the expanded Library eventually sold 48 million copies, in candy boxes, Woolworth's stores, and through an unsuccessful Book-of-the-Week Club. It also kick-started Scherman's publishing company. In 1926 he and his partners founded the Book-of-the-Month Club, which has made the vice of reading all too easy to practice.

Books are like a mirror. If an ass looks in, you can't expect an angel to look out.

– Arthur Schopenhauer, 19th-century German philosopher

21 · DESERT ISLAND ENDURABLE

What better volume than this – a book about books – to take along if you're cast away alone on an island? However, if you want further inspiration, consider the choices made by guests on *Desert Island Discs*, BBC Radio's longest-running record program. Host Roy Plomley launched this fantasy show in war-wracked London in 1942 (and yes, he later acknowledged that he really meant *deserted* island).

The idea was to invite prominent people to discuss which favorite recordings they'd like to be stuck with for the rest of their lives on a lonely isle. Often they chose spoken-word discs as well as music. After about 400 shows, Plomley thought of also asking them which single book (or other reading material) they would want along with them. So many guests requested a multiple-volume encyclopedia that the host got bored and eventually banned these reference works from the island.

Others, looking for a nice long read, asked for Marcel Proust's monumental 16-volume cyclic novel, *Remembrance of Things Past*, or Edward Gibbon's more modest six-volume *The Decline and Fall of the Roman Empire* – a request of Sir Terence Rattigan, the British drama-tist *(Separate Tables)*. The author Sir Sacheverell Sitwell wisely if greedily chose a bound volume of *War and Peace* and *Anna Karenina*. A resourceful London journalist, Anne Sharpley, wanted the British armed forces' official survival manual but, learning it was classified, she called up the American forces and got their manual, *The Raft*.

Some other responses:

Playwright **Noël Coward** and actress **Tallulah Bankhead**: *The Human Situation,* by Professor C. MacNeill Dixon. Coward, in his role as playwright, also selected the love scene from his own *Private Lives*, which he'd recorded with Gertrude Lawrence.

Actress/singer **Marlene Dietrich**: *The Story of Life*, by Constantine Paustovsky.

Actor **Jimmy Stewart**: a book of piano arrangements by jazz composer Dave Brubeck.

Director **Alfred Hitchcock**: the Continental train timetable, for fantasy journeys.

Field Marshal the Viscount Montgomery: his own *History of Warfare*.

Author **Richard Gordon** (nom de plume of the physician who created the comic *Doctor* books, which became such films as *Doctor at Sea*): *Michelin Guide to France*. As he said, "to enjoy all those meals without actually eating them would be very slimming."

Violinist **Yehudi Menuhin**: a recording of Dylan Thomas reading his own poem, "And Death Shall Have No Dominion."

Conductor **George Solti**: two spoken records, John Gielgud reading the Shakespearean sonnet, "When my love swears that she is made of truth," and Winston Churchill's wartime "blood, toil, tears, and sweat" speech.

Artist **David Hockney**: *Route 69*, a pornographic American novel by Floyd Carter.

22 · TARGET

As a service to critics of this book, here are some classic reviews of famous works, which they might want to read for stimulation before venting their spleen:

King Henry VI, Part III, William Shakespeare

> For there is an upstart crow, beautified with our feathers, that with his tiger's heart wrapped in a player's hide, supposes he is as well able to bumbast out a blank verse as the best of you; and being an absolute *Johannes fac totum*, is in his own conceit the only Shake-scene in a country.
>
> > – Robert Greene, the English author from whom Shakespeare borrowed his plot for *A Winter's Tale*

Little Nell, Charles Dickens

> One must have a heart of stone to read the death of Little Nell without laughing.
>
> > – Oscar Wilde

The Evil Genius, Wilkie Collins

> Is it too much to hope that Mr. Wilkie Collins may be remembered as the last really able novelist who shackled and crippled his genius, and worried his admirers almost into giving up reading him, by systematically cumbering his stories with what are called "plots"?
>
> > – George Bernard Shaw

Dawn, Theodore Dreiser

> Theodore Dreiser
> Should ought to write nicer.
>
> > – Dorothy Parker, *The New Yorker*

Abraham Lincoln (six-volume biography), Carl Sandburg

The cruellest thing that has happened to Lincoln since he was shot by Booth has been to fall into the hands of Carl Sandburg.

– Edmund Wilson

The Winds of War, Herman Wouk

This is not at all bad, except the prose.

– Gore Vidal

23 · DEPRESSANT

Six quite depressing things to ponder on the subject of books – and society:

1. In the 1830s, having had his first work of fantasy and a collection of poetry successfully published, Hans Christian Andersen tried to find a publisher for his first volume of fairy tales, *Eventyr*. When every publishing house in Copenhagen turned him down, he was forced to pay for its printing and distribution himself.

2. "Books are fatal: they are the curse of the human race."

   > – Benjamin Disraeli, the British statesman, author (of several lousy novels), and son of a literary critic.

3. During the 1950s the Church League of America – in a militant national campaign spearheaded by executive secretary Edgar C. Bundy – tried to declare *The Girl Scout Handbook* un-American (for reasons that defy rational explanation).

4. "Go and ask the lady who checks out the videos and ask her where the books are."

   – Roseanne, to her son, on the immensely popular TV series *Roseanne*.

5. At the time of writing, the hardcover edition of *The Bridges of Madison County* by Robert James Waller had been on the *New York Times* Best Sellers list for 144 weeks.

6. Salman Rushdie.

Six quite pleasant things to ponder on the subject of books – and society:

1. Jacopo Sannazaro, a 16th-century Italian who wrote three volumes of pungent epigrams, received one of the highest fees for a work of poetry when the citizens of Venice gave him 1,000 gold crowns for each of these six lines of verse (which read much better in the original Italian):

    > Neptune saw Venus on the Adria stand
    > Firm as a rock, and all the sea command,
    > "Think'st thou, O Jove?" said he, "Rome's walls excel?
    > Or that proud cliffe, whence false Tarpei fell?
    > Grant Tiber best, view both; and you will say,
    > That men did those, god these foundations lay."

2. Augustine Birrell, chief secretary of Ireland, wrote: "Any ordinary man can . . . surround himself with two thousand books . . . and thenceforward have at least one place in the world in which it is possible to be happy." After being forced to retire for failure to end the plotting that led to the Easter Rebellion of 1916, Birrell found his happiness in writing biographies of Charlotte Brontë and Andrew Marvell.

3. The Canadian media critic Robert Fulford says that the increase in handsome book jackets has made the world a prettier place: "They've improved astonishingly: Put a sample of 25 book jackets from 1975 beside the same number from 1995, and those from 1975 will appear to be the work of amateurs. Obviously, someone is worrying about quality."

4. The $18-billion-a-year American book industry is currently growing at a rate of eight percent annually.

5. At the time of writing, the softcover edition of the prize-winning, critically acclaimed novel *The Shipping News*, by E. Annie Proulx, had been on the *New York Times* Paperback Best Sellers list for 48 weeks.

6. Alice Munro.

This book is five inches wide and eight inches high.

"A big book is as bad as a great misfortune," said Callimachis, the head librarian at Alexandria, in what's now northern Egypt. It's no wonder he didn't like oversized volumes. Founded about 283 B.C., his library had 700,000 papyrus rolls, the largest collection of written material ever assembled before the invention of printing.

Perhaps the bulkiest book ever, in area, was a collection of engravings by the French artist and archaeologist Baron Dominique Denon. Displayed on a six-ton swiveling lectern in the Escorial monastery and palace near Madrid, and bound in yellow leather with brass clasps, it stood six feet high and four across.

Small is beautiful, if somewhat difficult to read. There was a Bible dated 1660 that was tinier than a fingernail. Another, now resting in the British Museum's Harleian Library, can slip into a walnut shell. The smallest bound printed book ever sold on the market – all 85 copies – was *Old King Cole*, published by England's Gleniffer Press in 1985 as a volume $1/25$ of an inch square. You need a pin to flip the pages.

Try bringing a laptop computer into the tub and reading an on-screen novel on CD-ROM. But if you still worry about reading a real book in the bath, for fear of water damage, take a leaf from *The Anatomy of Bibliomania*, Holbrook Jackson's 1930 work on the passion for books. He recalls a friend's story "that when he was in Athens, he met a learned German, who, he was credibly informed by a very amusing lady, was supposed to have a Homer printed on indiarubber, to read during his bath."

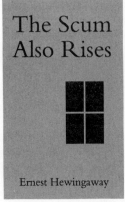

The Scum
Also Rises

Ernest Hewingaway

In the late spring of that year we lived in a cabin that looked out across the river and into the trees. There were fat trout in the water. There were fat people in boats trying to kill them. There were fat trees with sharp branches. They were pointed like banderillos' barbs in the corrida and they caught the old men's lines.

Consuela was beautiful as always. We were young and our hearts were as big as the Great Bulls we had run with in Pamplona. Our eyes were strong and the sky was washed clean, but we could see little of the new day. The window of the cabin was filthy.

"Consuela," I said.

"Ernest?" the woman asked, listening.

"It is time. Time to clean the windows."

"We have nothing."

It was quiet in the room. I said, "We have the *Times*, which said of my book: 'One is left at the end with nothing to digest.' That rag is good only for cleaning windows of scum."

"But how?"

"The hell with it. I will do it." And I tore the paper into strips and crushed them in my hands. I took the rough white Rioja wine that had turned to vinegar and splashed it on the glass. I washed the liquid off with the paper and as the window became clean I remembered I could also do this with the pages of a book.

Maybe, I thought, a book of the little Irish writer from Canada, Callaghan, who had bloodied my nose in Paris.

As your party begins to lose steam (well, okay, maybe your children's party), hold up this book and announce that you can walk right through one of its pages. Rather than ripping out the illustration below, you may want to have a photocopy handy. Then take a pair of scissors and cut along the lines, delicately open up the circle you've created, and step through. *Caution: Do not attempt with a computer page.*

Prop (noun): A property; in theater and film, an object that decorates a set.

> Books have never been more propish than on the PBS series *Masterpiece Theatre*, where the camera pans across their leather-bound beauty like a leering old man. Steve Martin sends all this up in the introduction to the video *Monty Python's Parrot Sketch Not Included*, where he holds a heavy tome like a weight and then attempts to replace it on the bookshelf – which is just painted, and falls apart.

Prop (verb): To support, hold up.

> Sir Edward Burne-Jones, the 19th-century Pre-Raphaelite English painter and decorator, argued that books were of absolutely no use to an artist except, as he said, "to prop up models in difficult positions."

There is no more literary a puzzle than the acrostic – in which the initial letters of each line form words – and perhaps none older. A 25-letter variant of the acrostic dating back to ancient Roman times was found in 1868 on a wall in Cirencester, the west England site of what was once Corinium.

The first acrostic of any note published in North America appeared in the *Saturday Review of Literature* in 1934. Elizabeth Kingsley had invented a game she called Double-Crostic which used a crossword puzzle grid but had a different set of instructions. The prototype set the tone for its successors by being unabashedly literary. It offered a list of definitions for words whose individual letters were then entered, by their corresponding numbers, in the squares of the grid. When filled in, the grid revealed a quotation from a well-known book. The initial letters of the words in the list spelled out the name of the author and the title of the work.

A decade earlier Simon and Schuster had released the first crossword puzzle book with resounding success – one order of 250,000 was the largest single book order of its time. And before her death in 1953, Elizabeth Kingsley had compiled 26 books containing 2,500 Double-Crostics of her own creation.

Here, to be solved again, is that historic Double-Crostic No. 1 (the answer is on page 136).

DIRECTIONS – To solve this puzzle, you must guess twenty-five words, the definitions of which are given in the column headed DEFINITIONS. The letters in each word to be guessed are numbered (these numbers appear at the beginning of each definition) and you are thereby able to tell how many letters are in the required word. When you have guessed a word each letter is to be written in the correspondingly numbered square on the puzzle diagram. When the squares are all filled in you will find (by reading from left to right) a quotation from a famous author. Reading up and down, the letters mean nothing! The black squares indicate ends of words; therefore words do not necessarily end at the right side of the diagram.

Either before (preferably) or after placing the letters in the squares you should write the words you have guessed on the blank lines which appear to the right in the column headed WORDS. The initial letters of this list of words spell the name of the author and the title of the piece from which the quotation has been taken.

48

DEFINITIONS   WORDS

I.   1-14-23-50-95. A perfume of roses.   I. _____

II. 145-6-28-90-137. Child's game played with cards and numbers.   II. _____

III. 97-8-79-146-98-61-75-77-76-32-27-19-133. Light as a feather.   III. _____

IV. 80-85-60-113-51-58-48. Held in high esteem; worshipped.   IV. _____

V.   81-172-31-84-24-176-65-89. Insubstantial.   V. _____

VI. 112-45-114-164-149-173-142-36. The business section of a city. VI. _____

VII. 144-102-2-63. Material for bandages.   VII. _____

VIII. 37-4-66-82-110-116-62. Upholstered backless seat.   VIII. _____

IX. 100-106-33-5-122-41-138-69-83-13-162-127. A Russian pianist.   IX. _____

X.   40-59-52-25. A drupe with a single seed.   X. _____

XI. 135-175-3-73. Movement of the ocean.   XI. _____

XII. 130-43-129-107-111-55-139-47. To alienate.   XII. _____

XIII. 15-121-92-136-101-39. A mighty hunter.   XIII. _____

XIV. 167-9-140-46-105. Artless; simple.   XIV. _____

XV. 119-54-104-17-153-34. Hebrew God.   XV. _____

XVI. 134-63-128-168-16-30. Flat, dark image.   XVI. _____

XVII. 155-125-78-148-143-165-158-56. Prejudiced (compound).   XVII. _____

XVIII. 12-96-120-11-7-170-150-21-68-174. Significant, unusual.   XVIII. _____

XIX. 87-141-171-161-67-20-10-126. Not propitious.   XIX. _____

XX. 177-99-152-163-108-115. Member of the tribe of Levi.   XX. _____

XXI. 42-88-26-159-49-91. Doodle dandy.   XXI. _____

XXII. 22-71-151-118-131-147-38-94-160-29. Watchword (Bibl.).   XXII. _____

XXIII. 109-86-132-124-72-117-123-178. Uttered a harsh sound.   XXIII. _____

XXIV. 157-44-93-53-166-18-35-103. Forceful.   XXIV. _____

XXV. 156-154-74-169-70-57. To stop the flow.   **XXV.** _____

49

A survey of 3,000 librarians for the 1993 Library Resources Exhibition in Birmingham, England, revealed a cornucopia of unusual bookmarks that had been left in returned books. Among them: an ancient jam sandwich, rashers of bacon, a kipper, and in Hengoed, Wales, used condoms.

Bookmarks – or bookmarkers, as they're more formally known – are wonderfully practical devices to protect a book while recalling where you left off in your reading. Placing a volume facedown cracks its spine; turning down the corner of a page defaces a book (the 18th-century English poet, dramatist, and clergyman Edward Young folded so many corners that, by the time he died, his library was full of dog-eared books that would no longer close).

One of the earliest records of a bookmark is the fringed silk specimen that Christopher Barker, a draper as well as a printer, presented to Queen Elizabeth in 1584 in gratitude for receiving the patent as Queen's Printer. By the 18th century the common bookmark was a slender silk ribbon bound into a book, a version still seen today in some reference works and a few distinguished tomes. Detached markers began surfacing in the 1850s, many of them homemade with embroidery and stitched-in watercolors. Three decades later they were more frequently made of paper and adorned with advertising for soap, patent medicine, and women's corsets. With World War I they became propaganda vehicles (in Britain a series of collectible bookmarks, like bubble-gum cards, pictured fighter planes and warships). Eventually more permanent versions appeared, of celluloid, silver, and tortoiseshell. Contemporary booksellers and publishers often use paper markers to promote their products (some Harlequin romances have a detachable cardboard bookmark that pushes the company's various series).

Many of us still use any handy object to mark our page, from toilet paper to bar coasters to eyeglasses – when Oxford University was bequeathed the library of the 17th-century English jurist and scholar John Selden, librarians found dozens of pairs of his spectacles in books where he'd misplaced them.

"The learned world," John Hill Burton writes in *The Book-Hunter*, "may very fairly be divided into those who return the books borrowed by them, and those who do not."

He tells of a writer friend, whom he disguises as Thomas Papaverius, who would not hesitate to seize another's copy of *Medea* or *The Republic*, bound in gilded and tooled leather: "True, the world at large has gained a brilliant essay on Euripides or Plato – but what is that to the rightful owner of the lost sheep?"

Other thoughts on this despicable practice:

> A friend thinks no more of borrowing a book now-a-days, than a Roman did of borrowing a man's wife; and what is worse, we are so far gone in our immoral notions on this subject, that we even lend it as easily as Cato did his spouse.
>
> – Leigh Hunt, English poet, critic, and friend of Shelley and Byron, in *Wedded to Books*.

> Never lend books, for no one ever returns them; the only books I have in my library are books that other folk have lent me.
>
> – Anatole France, French author (1844-1924), *My Friend's Book*.

Is there a better source for soothing lullabies than a storyteller who was raised in Ulster at a time when the Troubles were sundering Ireland? Alice Kane put her prodigious memory to good use in writing her incredibly detailed *Songs and Sayings of an Ulster Childhood*. Alice loved this sad little song that her mother sang to her; put any tune to it as you pacify your own little one:

> There was a wee lambie fell over a rock
> And when it fell over its leg it was broke,
> And all that the poor little lambie could do
> Was to lie and cry out "Billaloo, billaloo!"

Match these compelling first-person first lines with the books they should lure you into, if you haven't already read them (answers on page 136):

1. There were 117 psychoanalysts on the Pan Am flight to Vienna and I'd been treated by at least six of them.

2. The summer my father bought the bear, none of us was born – we weren't even conceived: not Frank, the oldest, not Franny, the loudest; not me, the next; and not the youngest of us, Lilly and Egg.

3. If you really want to hear about it, the first thing you'll probably want to know is where I was born, and what my lousy childhood was like, and how my parents were occupied before me, and all that David Copperfield kind of crap. . . .

4. My lifelong involvement with Mrs. Dempster began at 5:58 o'clock p.m. on the 27th of December, 1908, at which time I was ten years and seven months old.

5. Whether I shall turn out to be the hero of my own life, or whether that station will be held by anybody else, these pages must show.

6. Call me Jonah.

A. *Fifth Business*, Robertson Davies
B. *Cat's Cradle*, Kurt Vonnegut, Jr.
C. *David Copperfield*, Charles Dickens
D. *Catcher in the Rye*, J. D. Salinger
E. *Fear of Flying*, Erica Jong
F. *The Hotel New Hampshire*, John Irving

Abbie Hoffman, the American revolutionary of the 1960s and 1970s, wrote his autobiography and called it *Steal This Book*. So many of his readers did that it's often hard to find a copy in major libraries. However, no book (not even this one) is safe, no matter how friendly or holy or official the biblioklept – the book thief – may be.

Around the turn of the 17th century the English mathematician Sir Henry Savile wrote a letter introducing Sir Thomas Bodley, the English scholar and diplomat, to a fellow book-lover, Sir Robert Cotton. Savile knew just how much Bodley (who organized Oxford's Bodleian Library) loved books. "I give you faire warning," he advised Cotton, "that if you hold any booke so deare as that you would bee loath to have him out of your sight, set him aside beforehand."

In mid-century, in Italy, Roman Catholic Cardinal Francesco Barberini visited the painter Montier's intriguing library with Pamphilio, who would later become Pope Innocent X. Before they left, the cardinal suggested the artist check to see if any book was missing. One was: a small, rare volume. Montier accused Pamphilio of theft, and when the two men fell to fisticuffs, the book tumbled from the future pope's pocket. Once in power, Pamphilio expelled Barberini's family from Rome.

A century later, in France, the inspector general of French libraries, Guillaume Libri, was convicted for stealing books worth £20,000 and concealing his thefts with dummy volumes.

Of course, ordinary folk rip off books, too, although few go as far as Stephen Blumberg of Ottumwa, Iowa, who in 1991 received a 71-month sentence and a $200,000 fine for stealing about 28,000 rare books from libraries in North America.

It was called lucky dipping: the practice of opening a book at random, reading what your eyes first fell on, and believing that the words had some divine, prophetic, or otherwise consequential meaning. The ancient Greeks did this on occasion, flipping open Homer and Virgil. Christians continued the custom with the Bible, especially in France, until Louis I banned it in the eighth century, ordering "that no one shall presume to draw lots in the Psalms, or the Gospel or anywhere else, nor observe any divinations."

Of course, if you open this book haphazardly, your eyes will probably fall on the section titled Aphrodisiac.

Authors adore cats. Or enough do to have written a disgusting number of books about the feline descended from a prehistoric, weasel-like carnivore called *Miacis*. Aesop of mid-sixth century B.C. wrote such long-lived Greek fables as "The Cat, the Monkey, and the Chestnuts." Jean de la Fontaine's French fables of the 17th century included "The Cat, the Weasel, and the Rabbit," in which the wily old cat pretended deafness in settling an argument between the other animals and drew them close enough to eat them. In fairy tales, France's *Puss-in-Boots* and the English cat in *Dick Whittington* remain popular today. As do these fantasy felines: Edward Lear's Pussy-Cat, chumming around with the Owl, and Lewis Carroll's enigmatic Cheshire Cat.

Writers recognize the intrinsic cunning of cats. Montaigne, the 16th-century French essayist, wondered: "When I play with my cat, who knows if I am not a pastime to her more than she to me?" And they identify kindred qualities, as the 19th-century French poet Charles Baudelaire did: "Both ardent lovers and austere scholars, when once they come to the years of discretion, love cats, so strong and gentle, the pride of the household, who like them are sensitive to the cold, and sedentary." And his contemporary, Victor Hugo, like so many prominent French writers of the time, insisted on cats in his life – even constructing a chair shaped like a throne for one.

Classic children's books abound with cats, among them Beatrix Potter's *Samuel Whiskers*, Dr. Seuss's *Cat in the Hat*, Paul Gallico's *Jennie* and *Thomasina*, and T. S. Eliot's *Practical Cats*, which led to the everlasting Broadway musical, *Cats*. Nursery rhymes, too, would be the poorer without the creatures; one of the earliest recorded is "Ding, dong, bell / Pussy's in the well . . . ," which Shakespeare mentions in several plays.

Other esteemed authors, writing for adults, celebrate the cat with incautious praise. Percy Bysshe Shelley exulted: "O bard-like spirit! beautiful and swift!" Thomas Hardy grieved: "Pet was never mourned as you, Purrer of the spotless hue. . . ." Colette, like her French counterparts of the previous century, insisted: "Our perfect companions never have fewer than four feet." Perhaps no one was more adoring than the 18th-century English poet Christopher Smart, who eulogized his feline friend in a long poem: "For I will consider my cat Jeoffrey. / For he is the servant of the living God, / duly and daily serving him. . . ." But then, at the time, Smart was in London's Bedlam Asylum, where he was confined for religious mania.

Of course, some English poets have expressed an ambivalent attitude toward cats. Witness these lines from Thomas Gray's 18th-century "Ode on the Death of a Favourite Cat": "Not all that tempts your wand'ring eyes / And heedless hearts, is lawful prize; / Nor all that glistens, gold." Needless to say, the cat drowned attempting to spear the poet's goldfish.

The poet Shelley had a passion for making and sailing paper boats. Passion? We are talking *obsession*. He would linger by a body of water – England's Serpentine River, the pond in Kensington Gardens – until he'd exhausted all available paper. That included personal letters, once a £50 banknote, and yes, even books. As William Keddie recorded in 1894 in *Anecdotes Literary and Scientific*, "Of the portable volumes which were the companions of his rambles, and he seldom went without a book, the fly-leaves were commonly wanting – he had applied them as our ancestor Noah applied gopher-wood; but learning was so sacred in his eyes, that he never trespassed further upon the integrity of the copy; the work itself was always respected." Shelley's wife died by drowning in the Serpentine; he drowned while sailing on the Ligurian Sea in Italy.

Here's how to fold your own boat from a flyleaf of this book (or, if you prefer a larger vessel, use a conventional 8½ × 11-inch piece of paper): Fold the paper in half lengthwise. Open it. Fold it in half widthwise and leave it folded. Place the paper so that the folded edge is away from you. Fold both the top corners down so that they meet exactly at the lengthwise crease. You now have a shape like this:

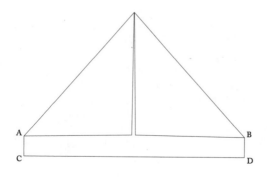

The rectangular ABCD portion at the bottom has two layers. Fold the top layer up along the line AB. Turn your paper over and fold the bottom rectangle up to match the top one. You now have what looks like a hat. Open the hat, give it a quarter turn, and flatten it into a diamond shape. (*Note*: The corners of the ABCD rectangles will be sticking up; tuck one underneath the other. Do that on both sides.) Now, fold one bottom point of the diamond up to the top. Turn your paper and fold the other bottom point in the same way. Now you have a triangular shape. Open it at the bottom, give it a quarter turn, and flatten it into a diamond shape. The two free points at the top of the diamond will become the prow and stern of the boat. Gently pull these points to the side, revealing the triangular sail inside the boat. To lengthen the sail and decrease the depth of the sides of the boat, first hold the prow point in one hand and gently pull up on the nearest base point of the sail; repeat with the stern.

Variant: Boat may also be worn as a silly hat.

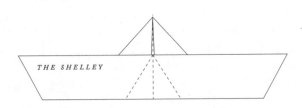

THE SHELLEY

Is it that now my inexperienced fingers
Must re-crease and re-fold a loftier sail,
As my dear friend by the Serpentine lingers,
Waits there in silence, watching while I fail?

– With apologies to Shelley's *The Revolt of Islam*

One of the principal qualities of the common book is its capacity to insulate. In place of a trivet or other stand of wood, metal, or plastic, the board-and-paper construction of this book affords protective properties against heat and cold that should not be dismissed in an emergency.

And if you wish to maintain the literary ambience of your kitchen, you might want to bake a favorite cake of Margaret Atwood, author of *The Handmaid's Tale*. The following recipe comes from a fund-raising book she edited, *The Canlit Foodbook*:

Bourbon Pecan Christmas Cake

2 cups	red candied cherries
2 cups	white seedless raisins
2 cups	bourbon
2 cups	butter or margarine
2 cups	white sugar
2 cups	dark brown sugar
8	eggs, separated
4½ cups	all-purpose flour
1½ tsp	baking powder
1 tsp	salt
2 tsp	ground nutmeg
½ cup	all-purpose flour
4 cups	pecan halves

Combine cherries, raisins, and bourbon in a bowl. Cover and refrigerate overnight. Drain, reserving bourbon. Cream the butter and add white and brown sugar; cream well. Add egg yolks and blend. Sift the 4½ cups of flour with baking powder, salt, and nutmeg. Add to butter mixture alternately with bourbon. Beat egg whites till stiff but not dry; fold into batter. Combine ½ cup of flour with pecans. Add to batter, along with cherries and raisins. Grease a 10-inch tube pan, line with wax paper, grease again, and dust with flour. Pour in batter to 1 inch of top. Pour rest of batter into a loaf pan similarly prepared. Bake the tube pan 4½ to 5 hours, the loaf pan 2½ to 3 hours, at 275° F. Remove; cool 15 minutes. Peel off paper and cool thoroughly on rack. Wrap cakes in cheesecloth, sprinkle with bourbon, wrap in foil, and seal with tape. Store 2 to 3 weeks minimum.

But what shall we say of those ghouls, chiefly in France, who scour the auction rooms, the booksellers' shops and the stalls, for choice and ancient bindings which they turn into boxes by gluing the pages together, cutting out the type area, and so translating books into receptacles for cigarettes, cigars, liqueurs, jewels, chocolates, bonbons, or note-paper.... They are no better than body-snatchers....

– Holbrook Jackson, *The Anatomy of Bibliomania*

To turn this or any book into a safe:

1. Holding a keen knife at right angles to the book, cut a few pages at a time; use a thin cutting board or heavy cardboard backing behind the pages. For tidy corners, cut away from them rather than toward them.

2. Glue the *edges* of the pages that form the inside hollow; use bookbinding glue or similar adhesive that, unlike white glue, does not crack when dry.

3. Place heavy books on the closed book safe overnight, or until the glue is dry.

4. For a more elegant look, glue silk or other cloth inside the hollow.

Locks of lovers' hair as treasured mementos and talismans went with soldiers into the Battle of Agincourt in 1415; beginning in the Middle Ages, couples exchanged them as tokens of friendship and fidelity. Literary folk were not immune: the romantic poet Lord Byron (1788-1824) had to surrender a lock to his hostess during a three-day visit to Spain and she reciprocated with one of her own, three feet long. When Byron broke off his affair with Lady Caroline Lamb, she nagged him for a bracelet of his hair; annoyed, the poet sent her one made from the pubic hair of a mutual woman friend.

In the Victorian era of the late 18th century, lovelocks adorned autograph albums, affixed to a page along with a verse from an admirer. Publishers created dummy-book boxes that would open to reveal individual sheets of paper on which every member of a family could tenderly mount swatches of hair. Today parents preserve their children's hair in baby albums, which sometimes include a special envelope to hold these hirsute souvenirs.

Great moments in book burning:

- Shih Huang Ti, emperor of China (246-210 B.C.), had all official histories and virtually every other book in the kingdom burned.

- The Islamic Caliph Omar seized Alexandria in 640 and burned one of its glories, the library. Apparently the 200,000 volumes heated the city's baths for six months. "If these writings of the Greeks agree with the Book of God, they are useless and need not be preserved," Omar reasoned. "If they disagree, they are pernicious and ought to be destroyed."

- In 1495 the Bonfires of the Vanities began in Florence as the Italian religious reformer Girolamo Savonarola burned irreplaceable works of art and manuscripts, including books by Dante, Boccaccio, and Ovid. (Three years later he and all his writings were burned in a Florentine piazza.)

- Robert Ainsworth, an 18th-century Englishman, was so engrossed in compiling his *Dictionary of the Latin Language* that his wife complained bitterly that he never spent time with her. Losing patience entirely as he was involved in the letter *S*, she threw all of his work into the fire. Ainsworth had the last *risus*: he managed to re-create the entire manuscript.

- During the War of 1812, the British sacked Washington, D.C., using the books in the Library of Congress to help burn most of the capital's public buildings, including the White House.

- Napoleon, who marched through books like his armies went through countries, used to speed-read many volumes in a day and toss those that didn't interest him into the fireplace (when he wasn't throwing them out the window of his railway carriage, to be picked up by passersby and sold to booksellers).

- In *Forty Years in My Bookshop*, Walter T. Spencer's 1923 memoir, he recalls a Captain Douglas who bought several hundred copies of a book called *Points of Humour* and then burned all but three he hoped would then be worth a small fortune. They never were.

- During World War II, the Nazis made bonfires of *verboten* books throughout Europe.

Books – the best antidote against the marsh-gas of boredom and vacuity.

– George Steiner, American critic

Once upon a lugubrious time, when the Compsons were moving beyond redemption, Benjy made a wager with his brother (Upton, the oldest, who would advance to Harvard and melancholy) that his shaggy, faltering hound was the equal of his (Upton's), although the hound of the brother was the scion of Benjy's mongrel and always hurrying, running, emulous. "By God," the brother said, "you take the two of them out in the big woods and no damn way that Old Hound is goin' to get back before the young 'un."

"I dont care how quick that pup is, my old ratter aint gonna lose," Benjy said.

They brought the dogs deep into the woods, where the unaxed wilderness solidified, and left them there snuffing and baying at a caged coon. When it began to get dark, the young hound left for home like a locomotive, in a line as straight as a track, crashing through the woodfern marsh and fungus-crusted willows, never veering, unremitting, running with the frenzy of a frantic squirrel. The Old Hound merely lifted its cold, drowsing eyes, blinked, reared up on its front legs, and with an ineffable regimental gait, a slow and wandering march, moved in his dogknowing way around and down hills, never up; out of the immitigable and melancholy cypress woods with their thick smell of rot and their hidden fairy tracks that he plodded along in his circumambience;

WILLIAM
FOLKLORE

THE
HOUND
IN A
HURRY

steadily, he moved, measuring his strength, the blood never coursing with any fever through his heart and brain.

the morning, when the dawn returned, the sun coming up red, the young pup was nowhere to be seen, caught in the ancient roots and thorns of the abiding woods, and the Old Hound, huffing, panting, dragged himself into the once-pasture around the house, lay down, blinked, and closed his cold, yellow eyes; and the moral of the story is: unhurried and unremitting prevails in the race

Humankind has chronicled the pestilent presence of the fly since the beginning of our known written record. The 14th clay tablet of the Mesopotamian series *Har-ra-Hubulla*, the oldest work of zoology we have, dates back 360 centuries and is based on lists from an even older Sumerian (non-Semitic) civilization. The tablet, written in a Semitic language, lists 11 insects – and 10 of them are flies, from toothed and trembling critters to the biting fly (probably the one now found in livestock stables).

And seldom has the fly had a fair shake in books. In commenting on ancient Jewish customs, the Talmud, composed from 200 to 500 A.D., says flatly: "A fly in food is offensive, and its presence there is ground for divorce." The Islamic prophet Mohammed advised: "If a fly falls into a container of one of you, have him remove all of it, then throw it away because certainly in one of its wings is remedy and in the other disease." And in Exodus of the Old Testament Moses warns: "Else if thou wilt not let my people go, behold, I will send swarms of flies upon thee, and upon thy servants, and upon thy people, and into thy houses: and the houses of the Egyptians shall be full of swarms of flies, and also the ground whereon they are."

The concept of the Book as Gift truly began to flourish in the England of the mid-19th century. That's when canny publishers released extravagantly illustrated and handsomely produced cloth- or morocco-bound books specially designed to be given away as presents. Some of the best artists of the period created woodcuts for what came to be called, because of their popularity in the 1860s, "sixties" books, or coffee-table books.

(If you would like to continue the commendable tradition of gift books, buy another copy of this one for your family or friends.)

49 · TWO-LETTER SCRABBLE GLOSSARY

(*Authorized Words*)

According to Joe Edley, associate director of the National Scrabble Association and two-time U.S. National Champion, 94 of those handy two-letter words have been authorized for tournament play of the word game invented by out-of-work architect Alfred Butts in 1931. *Ja* is not one of them; he says the German word for *yes* was officially disallowed in 1978. And although the 1994 edition of the British book, *Official Scrabble Words*, includes *qi*, Chinese for "life force," Edley says the word is not allowed in North American tournaments. However, the 1996 edition of *The Official Scrabble Players Dictionary* will be adding *yo*, which was a greeting on Philadelphia streets for generations before Sylvester Stallone popularized it in the *Rocky* movies.

AA	AD	AE	AG	AH	AI
AL	AM	AN	AR	AS	AT
AW	AX	AY	BA	BE	BI
BO	BY	DA	DE	DO	EF
EH	EL	EM	EN	ER	ES
ET	EX	FA	GO	HA	HE
HI	HM	HO	ID	IF	IN
IS	IT	JO	KA	LA	LI
LO	MA	ME	MI	MN	MO
MU	MY	NA	NE	NO	NU
OD	OE	OF	OH	OM	ON
OP	OR	OS	OX	OW	OY
PA	PE	PI	RE	SH	SI
SO	TA	TI	TO	UH	UM
UN	UP	US	UT	WE	WO
	XI	XU	YA	YE	

76

Oh, for some blessful spot
Where albums are no more,
Where no beloved one meets you
With an autographic lore.

– Jaded Maine youth, 1888

In the Greece of the first century B.C., Cicero recorded his pride at having the signature of Julius Caesar in his collection. But it was Germans in the 16th century who first popularized the collecting of people's names and messages handwritten in a special book, called the *Stammbuch* or *Album Amicorum*, with hand-painted coats of arms. As they were taken along by young people traveling or attending university, they evolved into albums with sketches and hand-cut silhouettes, painted flowers, and needlework. In North America publishers were printing autograph books in the 1820s, many with pages edged in gilt and adorned with scenes from steel engravings or flowers done in color lithography. Half a century later they were publishing books of verses "suitable for inscription in Albums, on all occasions."

Inevitably collectors started gathering signatures and signed letters of famous people (in 1986 Sotheby's auctioned an 1818 letter of Thomas Jefferson, in which he condemns anti-Semitism, for $360,000). Here are some interesting literary signatures to get you started on your own collection, and a blank page to add others:

William Shakespeare

Gustave Flaubert

Fyodor Dostoyevsky

Samuel Clemens/Mark Twain

Ernest Hemingway

F. Scott Fitzgerald

Long before the creators of movie ads began hunting down obscure favorable reviews or massaging famous critics' quotations to make a film sound more swell than it is, there were the writers of book blurbs.

Blurb – a word invented about 1907 by the American humorist Gelett Burgess – now means the promotional text on a dust jacket that both describes a book and offers testimonials to its worth. Book testimonials from notables were common in North America by the turn of the century; Teddy Roosevelt was so ardent a reader that publishers sent him as many books as possible in hope of getting the presidential stamp of approval.

It's not difficult to transform a lukewarm or rotten review into a glowing plug for an author's prose. Take, for instance, the critic Edmund Wilson's writing about W. H. Auden in 1952: "Mr. Auden himself has presented the curious case of a poet who writes an original poetic language in the most robust English tradition but who seems to have been arrested in the mentality of an adolescent schoolboy." Now, class, what would you quote in the blurb of the next edition of Auden's work? Of course: "original poetic language in the most robust English tradition. . . ."

For a more recent example, we have *1945*, the first novel of the U.S. Speaker of the House, Newt Gingrich. Hearing of the existence of this work of historical science fiction, Maureen Dowd of the *New York Times* wrote: "Now that I realize he can talk like Cotton Mather and write like Jacqueline Susann, I am eager to see how his sci-fi book comes out." ABC reporter Sam Donaldson said snidely, "This is an instant classic which will be draped athwart the Speaker's neck by his opponents in every election he runs in now."

So what, dear students, did Baen Books extract from these remarks of Gingrich's journalistic critics during the novel's national publicity campaign in the summer of 1995? Yes: "I am eager to see how his sci-fi book comes out." – Maureen Dowd. And, naturally: "An instant classic!" – Sam Donaldson.

On a bus or a plane, reading a book intently (or pretending to) can be the perfect device to forestall unwanted conversation with your seatmates. It helps, too, if you have a volume whose title makes them wary of engaging you in idle chitchat. One that might be a little hard to find now was mentioned in *Observations of Popular Antiquities* (circa 1800): *Pappe with an Hatchet, alias, a Fig for my Godsonne, or, crake me this Nutt, or, a Countrie Cuff, that is, a sound Box of the Eare for the Idiot Martin, to hold his Peace: seeing the Patch will take no warning; written by one that dares call a Dog a Dog.*

But more recent books, which have actually been published, include: *Shoes and Shit: Stories for Pedestrians*; *The Madam as Entrepreneur: Career Management in House Prostitution*; *New Guinea Tapeworms and Jewish Grandmothers*; *The Water of Life – A Treatise on Urine Therapy*; *Wife Battering: A Systems Theory Approach*; and *Suicide – Anyone?*

The reading of books provides plenty of reasons not to kill oneself. Here are half a dozen good ones:

> You think your pain and your heartbreak are unprecedented in the history of the world, but then you read.
>
> – James Baldwin

> Every man who knows how to read has it in his power to magnify himself, to multiply the ways in which he exists, to make his life full, significant, and interesting.
>
> – Aldous Huxley

> How many a man has dated a new era in his life from the reading of a book.
>
> – Henry David Thoreau

> Come, and take a choice of all my library;
> And so beguile thy sorrow.
>
> – William Shakespeare

> Reading is to the mind what exercise is to the body.
>
> – Sir Richard Steele

> We should read to give our souls a chance to luxuriate.
>
> – Henry Miller

This book – or almost any book, for that matter – can be transformed into an artwork by a brilliant bookbinder, who will usually retain the original covers while encasing the book in a design and with materials that both comment on and enhance the meaning of the words within.

In 1992 the City of Paris presented one of the most dazzling exhibitions of the art of modern bookbinding ever mounted. Eighteen French and seven foreign binders bound books in the city's Historic Library collection, some dating from the 16th century. Among the finest works were those of a pioneer of nonconventional binding, England's Philip Smith, who considers bookbinding an art rather than a decorative craft. For the covers of *Moby Dick,* he sculpted many layers of shagreen leathers, hand-painted with acrylics, and used balsa wood for the casing, or box, that holds the book, which is adorned with images of whales and Captain Ahab. Smith has been a role model for France's audacious Daniel Knoderer, whose bindings explode out of a book's normal boundaries. He wields such materials as plastic cutlery, Lego pieces, and transistor parts, as well as classical calfskin. *The Danse of the Infidels,* a collection of jazz pianist Bud Powell's scores, incorporated piano keys in its creatively chaotic design; *The Boomerang Kickback*, by Michel Butor, was trapezoidal in shape and included real boomerangs.

55 · JEWELRY

About 1895 a Glasgow publisher printed a book called *Witty, Humorous and Merry Thoughts* in an edition that was small enough to enclose in a locket that was small enough to nest in the palm of the hand. They were sold together as a piece of jewelry.

You can make your own jewelry – in this case, a necklace – by photocopying the pattern below and following these steps:

1. Use the pattern to cut out several pieces of paper – the prettier or more interesting, the better. The number of pieces will depend on how large you want to make the necklace.

2. Coat one side of each piece of paper with glue.

3. Starting from the wide end, and with the glued side up, roll each piece around a wooden matchstick, or something equally rigid and of similar circumference, to form cylindrical shapes that will be fatter in the middle than on the ends. Let these "beads" dry.

4. String the beads on an attractive thin cord. You may want to shellac them first for durability.

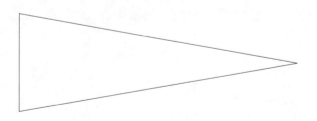

This book might amuse you the next time there's nothing good on your hotel television and you don't want to pay for an in-room movie. Failing that, you could always check the dresser drawer to see if there's a Bible to browse. In 1899 three commercial travelers in Janesville, Wisconsin, founded Gideons International, an interdenominational religious organization of Christian business and professional men. Nine years later Gideons began placing the King James Version of the Bible in hotel rooms. Less than nine decades later it has placed 36.6 million New Testaments, all but 10 percent of them aimed at travelers who have found room at an inn.

Highlights of advice on sex from influential books throughout history:

1542: "Lettyse doth extynct veneryous actes [lettuce kills a man's sexual desire]." – *A Dyetary of Helth (the boke for a good husbande to lerne)*, Andrew Boorde. Rabbits, ignore.

1560: Italian anatomist Gabriello Fallopius, who discovered fallopian tubes and conceived a linen condom, published a book in which he advised lovers to wash their genitals after sex to avoid infections. The title: *De Morbo Gallico* (*The French Disease*).

1887: *Spermatorrhea*, by J. L. Milton (no relation to *the* Milton, one trusts), was in its 12th edition, still suggesting that boys be placed in cages studded with spikes to stop them from the evil of masturbation.

1926: Dutch gynecologist Theodoor van de Velde released *Ideal Marriage*, which left a lot of couples wanting with its definition of "normal" sexual intercourse as that "which takes place between two sexually mature individuals of opposite sex; which excludes cruelty and the use of artificial means of producing voluptuous sensations; which aims directly or indirectly at the consummation of sexual satisfaction, and which, having achieved a certain degree of stimulation, concludes with the ejaculation – or emission – of the semen into the vagina, at the nearly simultaneous culmination of sensation – or orgasm – of both partners."

1953: "Although we may use orgasm as a measure of the frequency of female activity, and may emphasize the significance of the orgasm as a source of physiologic outlet and of social interchange for the female, it must always be understood that we are well aware that this is not the only significant part of a satisfactory sexual relationship." – *Sexual Behavior in the Human Female*, Alfred C. Kinsey and colleagues.

In recent years the cellulose found in books and newspapers has been used to make a mash for cows and other farm animals. A variation: a 17th-century account tells of one farmer who, in treating his sick cattle, fed them water in which had been soaked a supposedly miraculous text – the very rare *Book of Durrow*. This text dates back to the seventh century, a time when the Venerable Bede, an English historian, had claimed a cure with medicine made from the scrapings of holy books.

North America has a multitude of bookstores where you can swap this book when you're finished – or have other reasons for getting rid of it. But to find the broadest selection of books to trade in one place, you might make a pilgrimage to Wales or Continental Europe.

In 1962 Richard Booth began turning a Welsh town into the world's largest trading center of secondhand books, where at least 40 shops stock antiquarian and other used volumes. The outrageous bookseller crowned himself King of Hay-on-Wye, moved into a castle, and committed other self-publicizing acts that helped make him millions of pounds from books. The first book village across the Channel was Redu, Belgium, where in 1981 Noel Anselot opened an antiquarian shop, soon to be joined by 50-plus colleagues. Booth and Anselot then helped retired bookbinder Michel Braibant launch *un village du livre* in Montolieu, southern France, where serious European book collectors and curiosity-seekers flock to 20 or more bookstores scattered around a comely community of red-tiled, golden-stone structures.

"We live in the New Age of reason, science and artificial light," writes Dr. Joseph Gold in *Read for Your Life*. "The primal fears of darkness, savagery and the unknown are being swept away with the rain forests. Not so, says the horror writer. Look inside yourself, look at how little it takes to scare you, look at your own anger, greed, frustration and sadism, and having looked, respect the power and beware."

Do you doubt these words? Read this excerpt from Edgar Allan Poe's 1846 classic, "The Cask of Amontillado," in which the narrator wreaks revenge on Fortunato by tricking him into visiting his wine vaults down in the bone-strewn catacombs – where he chains his victim and begins walling him up behind a niche. Read it, and try to erase the scene from your memory:

> I had scarcely laid the first tier of masonry when I discovered that the intoxication of Fortunato had in a great measure worn off. The earliest indication of this was a low moaning cry from the depth of the recess. It was *not* the cry of a drunken man. There was then a long and obstinate silence. I laid the second tier, and the third, and the fourth; and then I heard the furious vibrations of the chain. The noise lasted for several minutes, during which, that I might hearken to it with more satisfaction, I ceased my labours and sat down upon the bones. When at last the clanking subsided, I resumed the trowel, and finished without interruption the fifth, the sixth, and the seventh tier. The wall was now nearly upon a level with my breast. I again paused, and holding the flambeaus over the mason work, threw a few feeble rays upon the figure within.
>
> A succession of loud and shrill screams, bursting suddenly from the throat of the chained form, seemed to thrust me violently back. For a brief moment I hesitated, I trembled. Unsheathing my rapier, I began to grope with it about the

recess; but the thought of an instant reassured me. I placed my hand upon the solid fabric of the catacombs, and felt satisfied. I reapproached the wall; I replied to the yells of him who clamoured. I re-echoed, I aided, I surpassed them in volume and in strength. I did this, and the clamorer grew still.

It was now midnight, and my task was drawing to a close. I had completed the eighth, the ninth, and the tenth tier. I had finished a portion of the last and the eleventh; there remained but a single stone to be fitted and plastered in. I struggled with its weight; I placed it partially in its destined position. But now there came out of the niche a low laugh that erected the hairs upon my head. It was succeeded by a sad voice, which I had difficulty in recognizing as that of the noble Fortunato. . . .

"For the love of God, Montresor!"

"Yes," I said, "for the love of God!"

Don't fret that by buying this book you have necessarily contributed to the destruction of a tree. In North America trees are generally not cut down to make paper; there's so much money in using solid wood for timber products that the forest companies wouldn't waste perfectly good trees to create the pulp for paper. So where does the paper come from? Sixty-six percent of it is the residue from sawmill operations, such as wood chips that would otherwise be discarded; another 18 percent is waste paper. Only 16 percent is directly from roundwood, and much of that is from private woodlot owners and farmers thinning their woodlands.

63 · WEAPON

In Charlotte Brontë's *Jane Eyre*, the 10-year-old heroine is set upon by her stout older cousin, John: "when I saw him lift and poise the book and stand in act to hurl it, I instinctively started aside with a cry of alarm: not soon enough, however; the volume was flung, it hit me, and I fell, striking my head against the door and cutting it. The cut bled, the pain was sharp: my terror had passed its climax; other feelings succeeded."

In real life the corpulent and ill-dressed Dr. Samuel Johnson of dictionary fame once flung a large rare volume at his bookseller employer. It hit the man in the head and toppled him. Johnson stepped over the body, saying, "Lie there, thou lump of lead."

Anthony Trollope noted that his father often felled him with an oversized Bible for being lazy. "As missiles," Holbrook Jackson drolly observes about big Bibles in *The Anatomy of Bibliomania*, "they are widely appreciated, lending themselves as they do both by reason of their size and shape to sudden precipitation at an offending head."

All that the world's libraries need is yet another book. The largest, the U.S. Library of Congress (founded in 1800 in Washington, D.C.), already has more than 98.6 million items in its collection, with nearly 600 miles of shelving in the 2.85 million square feet of its three main locations, and 350,000 square feet at another six sites. About one-quarter of the collection is books, in at least 468 languages.

Glory be to God for dappled things –
For skies of couple-color as a brinded cow;
For rose-moles all in stipple upon trout that swim;
Fresh-firecoal chestnut-falls; finches' wings;
Landscape plotted and pieced – fold, fallow, and plough;
And áll trádes, their gear and tackle and trim.
All things counter, original, spare, strange;
Whatever is fickle, freckled (who knows how?)
With swift, slow; sweet, sour; adazzle, dim;
He fathers-forth whose beauty is past change:
Praise him.

– Gerard Manley Hopkins (1844-1899)

Words intoxicate. When ill health forced Thomas Hood, the 19th-century poet/humorist, to imbibe nothing stronger than "the drink that drowns kittens," he consoled himself with "the champagne of Molière, the Monte Pulciano of Boccaccio, the hock of Schiller, and the sherry of Cervantes," and became "intellectually elevated with Milton, a little merry with Swift, rather jolly with Rabelais" – whose magnificent ribald romance *Pantagruel* he found "equal to the best gruel with rum in it." And it was an unidentified pamphleteer a century earlier who, in *A Project for the Destruction of Printing and Bookselling*, had recommended barreling and bottling books: "a cellar of books would be more invitingly absorbable than a library."

The Big Beach Books of the Past Decade – the top, often mindless, plump yet portable paperbacks for women and men, from the *New York Times* Paperback Best Sellers list at the height of each summer:

1985: *"…And Ladies of the Club,"* Helen Hooven Santmyer. Chronicle of an Ohio hamlet from 1868 to 1932. *The Haj,* Leon Uris. One man's experience in the wars of the Holy Land.

1986: *Lucky,* Jackie Collins. The heiress of a crime lord versus the heiress of a shipping tycoon. *Lake Woebegon Days,* Garrison Keillor. Yarns about life in a small Minnesota town.

1987: *Wanderlust,* Danielle Steel. A rich orphan comes of age as she travels the world. *Red Storm Rising,* Tom Clancy. The West tries to stave off the Russians in World War III.

1988: *Weep No More, My Lady,* Mary Higgins Clark. Love and murder at a swank California health spa. *Patriot Games,* Clancy. The CIA's Jack Ryan battles terrorists in England, Ireland, and America.

1989: *Zoya,* Steel. One woman's story, from St. Petersburg during the Russian Revolution to contemporary New York. *The Cardinal of the Kremlin,* Clancy. The CIA's Jack Ryan races to the rescue of an American secret agent.

1990: *While My Pretty One Sleeps,* Clark. The murder of a gossip writer in New York. *Clear and Present Danger,* Clancy. The CIA's Jack Ryan fights Colombian drug lords.

1991: *Lady Boss*, Collins. A woman schemes to get control of a movie studio. *Sullivan's Sting*, Lawrence Sanders. The ordeals of a female cop assigned to track down a Florida con man.

1992: *The Duchess*, Jude Devereaux. An American woman, in Scotland to marry a duke, finds a mysterious stranger more attractive. *The Sum of All Fears*, Clancy. Middle Eastern terrorists edge the world to the brink of nuclear war, and a floundering president may not be able to cope.

1993: *Scruples Two*, Judith Krantz. Continuing the story of the crowd that frequents an ultra chic Beverly Hills store. *The Firm*, John Grisham. A young lawyer learns that his firm is engaged in secret, possibly illegal activities.

1994: *The Client*, Grisham. Just before he kills himself, a lawyer reveals a deadly secret to an 11-year-old boy. *Without Remorse*, Clancy. John Kelly tries to rescue prisoners held in North Vietnam.

1995: *The Chamber*, Grisham. A lawyer represents a racist who is on death row for his part in a 1967 bombing. *The Stone Diaries*, Carol Shields. The journey of a woman from childhood to motherhood through old age.

Samuel Butler, working in the British Museum's reading room on *Erewhon* and other Utopian satires, auditioned different-sized books to use as a sloped writing desk. After many weeks, he found the perfect desk, a large volume called *Lives of Eminent Christians* – only to have it go missing on his next visit. As a substitute, *Corpus Ignatianum* was too skinny. *Magnalia* was big enough, except the binding was ugly. Finally he found an acceptable replacement, another inspirational tome, entitled *Cyclopoedia of Moral and Religious Anecdote*.

The Palm Springs sun blazed through the tall windows of the hacienda on to the gleaming white walls of the lavishly appointed exercise room, glancing off the equally luxurious lap pool where the blonde woman was ensconced on a floating divan. She lay quietly, as still as a statue in the Louvre. Tangerine purred as she remembered the night she had just spent with Max Palliser. The night . . . and half of the morning . . . and he would be here now if the studio hadn't sent a plane for him. Her long body was still tingling from the sweet punishment it had taken. She was nude except for a filmy peignoir that did nothing to hide her soft curves. Everything about Tangerine Taylor was soft . . . yet firm . . . like a mango turning ripe. She was no idiot. She hadn't spent her last large dividend cheque on the tummy-tuck for nothing. "You're so . . . exquisite," Max had said, gazing at her slim waist, her newly smooth stomach, glistening with

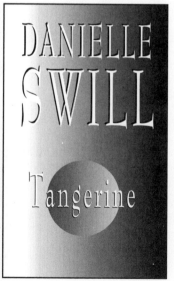

the afterglow of their desire and her nongreasy moisturizer. He looked serious as he had lifted her slender hand. . . .

Her hand! Now she thought with horror about how chipped her nails had been. And Warren would be here in an hour. Paddling to the edge of the pool, she pulled herself on to the warm tiles and picked up the cell phone she was never without. "Molly, bring me my nail polish kit, thank you," she said when a female voice answered. Within moments, her young brunette assistant, plump and efficient, arrived with the rosewood box that displayed polishes in colors to match any outfit, any mood. Tangerine dismissed her with a quick smile. Sometimes she wanted to do her own nails. But what shade today? There were so many. Perhaps . . . no . . . there! Berry Burst. Oh my God, the silly girl hadn't brought the lap tray. She must be still mooning over that older Polish woman who had dumped her. Tangerine looked around a little desperately and she saw a paperback lying beside the lounge chair. Which one . . . ? Oh, just Jacqueline's latest. . . . Well, she'd make better use of it this way than reading it. She pressed her left hand flat on the tacky-looking front cover and began polishing one sleek, perfectly shaped nail. . . .

If you live in the country, have your vegetables gathered from the garden at an early hour, so that there is ample time to make your search for caterpillars, &c. These disagreeable additions need never make their appearance on table in cauliflowers or cabbages, if the vegetable in its raw state is allowed to soak in salt and water for an hour or so.

That genteelly delivered counsel, still perfectly appropriate for use today, comes from *Beeton's Book of Household Management*, which Isabella Mary Beeton of London published in 1859. With its precise listing of ingredients, natural history of animals and vegetables, and detailing of servants' duties, the fat illustrated work was the first to target England's upwardly mobile middle classes. "I have always thought that there is no more fruitful source of family discontent than a housewife's badly-cooked dinners and untidy ways," wrote the young Mrs. Beeton. Her book, a product of four years' labor, even dealt with medical matters and "Management of Children." Unfortunately its bulk made it a bit awkward to handle – "dropped once in the kitchen," Eric Quayle points out in *The Collector's Book of Books*, "it would inevitably split its hinges and spring sections of text." The author herself died at 28 during the birth of her fourth child. But revised editions of *Mrs. Beeton's*, which preserve some of the original text, continue to be published.

Here are some names and addresses of literary folk to get you started on a tony address book, with some space for your own list:

Maya Angelou
3240 Valley Road
Winston-Salem, NC 27106

John Le Carré
Tregiffian, St. Buryan
Penzance, Cornwall
England

Janelle Taylor
2387 Louisville Road
Appling, GA 30802

Norman Mailer
142 Columbus Heights
Brooklyn, NY 11201

William F. Buckley, Jr.
150 East 35th St.
New York, NY 10016

Shirley MacLaine
25200 Old Malibu Road
Malibu, CA 90265

Dick Francis
Blewbury, Didcot
Oxfordshire OX11 9NH
England

J. D. Salinger
RR 3, Box 176
Cornish Flat, NH 03746

Jack Higgins
Septembertide
Mont de la Rocque
Jersey, Channel Islands
United Kingdom

Gloria Steinem
118 East 73rd St.
New York, NY 10021

Books of quotations in English have been around at least since 1799, when D. E. Macdonnel published *A Dictionary of Quotations chiefly from Latin and French translated into English.* The most famous such collection is still *Bartlett's Familiar Quotations*, compiled by John Bartlett, who ran the University Bookstore near Harvard around the mid-1850s. Although he'd quit school at 16, Bartlett was such a fount of other people's words that students were forever hitting him up for apt quotes for their course work. His commonplace book of quotations from 169 sources – mostly poetic and biblical, only four of them by women – became the first self-published paperback *Bartlett's* in 1855. It hasn't been out of print since.

Some quotations to quote about quotations during your next literary salon (none but the last appears in *Bartlett's*):

> **Quotation,** n. The act of repeating erroneously the words of another. The words erroneously repeated.
>
> – Ambrose Bierce, *The Devil's Dictionary*

> I have laboriously collected this cento out of diverse writers. I have wronged no authors but given every man his own. . . . Bees do little harm and damage no one in extracting honey; I can say of myself, whom have I injured?
>
> – Robert Burton, *Anatomy of Melancholy*

> One advantage there certainly is in quotation, that if the authors cited be good, there is at least so much worth reading in the book of him who quotes them.
>
> – Samuel Johnson

To be apt in quotation is a splendid and dangerous gift. Splendid, because it ornaments a man's speech with other men's jewels; dangerous, for the same reason.

– Robertson Davies

I love [quotations] because it is a joy to find thoughts one might have, beautifully expressed with much authority by someone recognizedly wiser than oneself.

– Marlene Dietrich

I have gathered a posie of other men's flowers, and nothing but the thread that binds them is my own.

– John Bartlett

A codfish opened up in the Cambridge, England, market back in 1626 had a slime-covered book wrapped in sailcloth in its gut. The author of the religious work was John Frith, who had been imprisoned in a fish cellar in Oxford (where several of his cellmates had died from the fumes of bad fish) and who was later burned at the stake in 1533. The book was reprinted under a new title, *Vox Piscis* – translated into English as *The Book-Fish* – and redesigned with a woodcut picturing the book inside the fish in a market stall.

Twenty-four inches of books equals the required eight inches of protective steel for a fallout shelter, which nuclear families once built to huddle in during the chilliest days of the Cold War. That thickness of a wall of books in an improvised shelter will block out 90 percent of the gamma radiation from a radioactive bomb.

The finest compliment you can pay the author of this book is to buy it. He will earn a royalty on each copy sold – a pittance of a return, truly, for the toil he has invested in its creation. He takes comfort, however, in the fact that others, some of them his betters, have received as little for their labors.

A sampling of well-known works and the financial rewards they repaid their authors, expressed in the legal tender of their eras:

- *Hamlet* (circa 1600), William Shakespeare: £5.

- *Paradise Lost* (blank-verse poem in 12 books, 1667), John Milton: £5.

- *Tom Jones* (the *print* version, 1749), Henry Fielding: £700.

- *Dictionary of the English Language* (nine years' work, appearing in 1755), Samuel Johnson – who said "No man but a blockhead ever wrote, except for money": £1,575.

- *The Vicar of Wakefield* (1766), Oliver Goldsmith – who was more successful as a playwright and one-book novelist than as a physician: £60.

- *Northanger Abbey* (sold in 1803, but bought back by the author's family and first published in 1818 after her death), Jane Austen: £10.

- *Phineas Finn* (the *eighth* of the author's successful novels, 1869), Anthony Trollope – who kept his day job with the Irish Post Office: £3,200.

- *To the Finland Station: The Writing and Acting of History* (1940), Edmund Wilson: an advance against royalties of $1,700 – or less than $300 a year for each of the six years it took the distinguished American critic to write his ode to the Russian Revolution.

- *Delta of Venus*, (erotica written for an American book collector's wealthy male client, 1940-41), Anaïs Nin – the Paris-born diarist and pal of Henry Miller: $1 a page.

- *The Fortunate Pilgrim* (1964), Mario Puzo: $1,500 advance (according to publisher Walter Zacharius, who says this first, autobiographical novel "became a big winner for us" after Puzo became famous for *The Godfather*).

The ancient riddles were sometimes considered a divine code, posed by oracles and comprehended only by those with secret wisdom. With the birth of the printing press, collections of riddles were among the first and most popular books; one, called *Amusing Questions*, was published in 1511 by an Alsatian printer in London with the amusingly apt name of Wynkyn de Worde. *The Exeter Book*, with riddles written in the 10th century or earlier, came to rest in England's Exeter Cathedral. And the oral history of some old fairy tales presents classic riddlelike situations, such as the following one. If you can't figure out the answer (in, say, a month), return to Use No. 1 (page 7) to see how to solve it; the answer is spelled out in Use No. 98 (page 136).

> A commoner in the Kingdom was beloved of everyone, including the birds and animals. The jealous King was displeased by the man's popularity and imprisoned him. His announcement that his subject would be put to death caused such a public outcry that he was obliged to give the man a chance to live. "I will present you with two pieces of paper," the King told him. "One will be marked *Life* and the other *Death*. You have it in your power to choose one or the other from a chalice and save your own life." But the King was being deceitful. As the commoner sat in his cell, contemplating his fate, a bird flew in the window and said that the King had marked both pieces of paper with the word *Death*. The good man swallowed hard and asked himself how he could out-trick the trickster. The next day, in a public ceremony for all to see, the King held out the chalice and the man chose one piece of paper. What did he do to save his own life?

Tonino Benacquista is a European *série noire* thriller writer, whose works include such titles as *The Madonna of the Sleeping Car.* He offers an appropriately dark literary tale about the cigarette: how his father came to smoke Plato. A soldier imprisoned in Albania, Benacquista Senior had only the remnants of tobacco in his pocket, along with a match and a copy of the Greek philosopher's *Cratylus* – a page of which he used to roll his own and have a thoughtful smoke.

Here are but a handful of the many useful or euphonious words that have fallen out of the English language and should be reinstated forthwith:

Aeipathy (noun): Long-simmering passion (pronounced *eye-IP-athy*), from the Greek *aiei* for *always* and *pathos* for *feeling*.

Backfriend (noun): A false friend, an enemy posing as a friend (15th century).

Comperendinate (verb): To postpone or procrastinate day by day (17th to 18th centuries; from the Latin *com* and *perendie*, day after tomorrow).

Gracile (adjective): Gracefully slender; sometimes used to describe literary style, from the Latin *gracilis* for *slender* (still in standard dictionaries but not in use).

Sparple (verb): To run off in different directions; to spread rumors (14th to 17th century); also, *disparple*, *sperple*, etc.

Whiffler (noun): One who smokes tobacco; used snidely (17th to 19th century); or one who is evasive.

(Literally)

The 17th-century Danish patriot Theodore Reinking had to eat his words after publishing a book critical of the Swedes who had assumed control of Denmark. After languishing in jail for several years, he was offered an alternative: to lose his head or to gain his release only by dining on his book page by page. He chose the latter course, converting the pages into a sauce of his own creation to wash down his heated prose.

In 1986 the London *Daily Telegraph* reported a more contemporary case of the edible book: "Howard Nolan, 20, an undergraduate at Brasenose College, Oxford, yesterday finished eating the 566 pages of a copy of the University Examination Statutes, which he began six days earlier."

(*For the Soul*)

"Some books are to be tasted," wrote philosopher and statesman Francis Bacon (1561-1626), "others to be swallowed, and some few to be chewed and digested. . . ." Others to be *devoured*. In 1791 James Boswell's *The Life of Samuel Johnson* described how the lexicographer had a book at hand even while eating: "He kept it wrapped in the tablecloth in his lap during the time of dinner, from an avidity to have one entertainment in readiness, when he should have finished another; resembling (if I may use so coarse a simile) a dog who holds a bone in his paws in reserve, while he eats something else which has been thrown to him."

A final thought from 20th-century novelist E. M. Forster: "Books have to be read (worse luck it takes so long a time). It is the only way of discovering what they contain. A few savage tribes eat them, but reading is the only method of assimilation revealed to the West."

In Claude Zidi's 1985 French film, *Les Ripoux* (released in North America as *My New Partner*), the veteran cop played by Philippe Noiret advises his fledgling sidekick about extracting quick confessions: "Kicking and beating leave marks. But there's one surefire method. Watch me." And he picks up the nearest book – in this case, a phone book – and slams it down on the head of a suspect.

In France there's inevitably a book handy. Who else but the French could have made a film like *La Lectrice* (1988), in which the actress Miou-Miou imagines herself as the heroine of a story she is reading to her boyfriend? Naturally, the "heroine" is a professional reader who becomes embroiled in the lives of her many clients. In fact, a letter writer to the *New York Times* has noted, discussing movie clichés, "In French films, there is always at least one scene in which a character is reading a book. In most American movies, there are no books. (The exception, *Pulp Fiction*, an American homage to French cinema, proves the rule.)"

Another exception to the above rule in Use No. 81 is Martin Scorsese's black comedy *After Hours* (also 1985), in which the hero is in a restaurant, seemingly engrossed in rereading Henry Miller's *Tropic of Cancer*. "I love that book," says the attractive blonde woman at the next table. "This is not a book. This is a prolonged insult. A gob of spit in the face of art. A kick in the pants to truth, beauty, God – something like that. That's all I remember." And then she joins him at his table.

In *Better Than Life*, French writer Daniel Pennac's passionate hymn to reading, he enthuses:

> Few objects inspire a feeling of absolute ownership the way books do. Once we get our hands on them, books become our slaves. Slaves, yes, for they are alive, yet no one would dream of freeing them, for their flesh is fashioned from dead trees. As objects of our outlandish love, they suffer terrible abuse. How do I abuse thee? Let me count the ways. I dog-ear your pages (I know it's a sin, but that way I never lose my place). I put my coffee cup on your cover and leave little halos there. . . . Forlorn childhood treasures that no one reads anymore have been exiled to a cottage where no one ever goes. And all those others in the second-hand shops, slaves auctioned over and over again. . . .

Babette Deggan of Vancouver, British Columbia, who was raised in Paris, tells the story of attending her mother's funeral in 1984: "The whole family is gathered at the cemetery. Then my two great-cousins arrive in a Bentley. They're twins who have worked their way up to being generals in the French Army. Both of them stand about one-meter-six [less than five feet]. One of them is driving – I can't tell one from the other – and when he opens the door I see he's sitting on a book to help him see over the dashboard as he drives. It's a painful moment. And I get the giggles."

By the middle of the 13th century, after professional scribes had taken over from monks in copying manuscripts, private individuals could collect books for their own use and resell them for profit.

Inevitably collecting became a mania for some. Richard Heber, a 19th-century collector, had to buy seven extra houses in England and Europe to hold his books, which may have numbered 300,000 (who knows exactly?). Heber thought nothing of traveling several hundred miles in a single day to seek out a single book. He believed that the wise collector should buy three copies of each volume: "One he must have for show copy . . . another he will require for his own use and reference; and unless he is inclined to part with this, which is very inconvenient, or risk the injury of his best copy, he must needs have a third at the service of his friends."

If only all bookmen were so gracious. In *The Book-Hunter* John Hill Burton tells of the Irish collector who had the only two copies of a book called *Rout upon Rout, or the Rabblers Rabbled*. When an important scholar asked to see it, for even just a few minutes, he refused, saying: "I might as well ask him to make a present of his brains and reputation."

In bold contrast was the California railway tycoon Henry E. Huntington, who early in this century began collecting handsome specimens of the works of giants – among them, poet William Blake – and first editions of such unproven writers as H. G. Wells. He bequeathed his books to be studied by everyone: one of the world's grandest collections of rare works of literature and history now rests in the Huntington Library in San Marino, California, which includes the finest edition of Chaucer's *Canterbury Tales* and the original manuscript of Benjamin Franklin's account of his early life, one of the best autobiographies ever written.

The soporific qualities of classic literature were never more keenly acknowledged than in a Columbia University survey of the world's most boring Great Books. College-educated readers polled by its bulletin, *The Pleasures of Publishing,* named these top 10 sleep-inducers:

1. *The Pilgrim's Progress* (1678), John Bunyan

2. *Moby Dick* (1851), Herman Melville

3. *Paradise Lost* (1667), John Milton

4. *The Faerie Queene* (1590), Edmund Spenser

5. *The Life of Samuel Johnson* (1791), James Boswell

6. *Pamela* (1740), Samuel Richardson

7. *Silas Marner* (1861), George Eliot

8. *Ivanhoe* (1819), Sir Walter Scott

9. *Don Quixote de la Mancha* (the satire was published in two parts, 1605, 1615), Miguel de Cervantes

10. *Faust* (the dramatic poem, also in two parts, 1808, 1832), Johann Wolfgang von Goethe

For a taste of just how tedious (and chauvinistic) the first-prize winner is, consider this passage from *The Pilgrim's Progress, From this world to That which is to come: Delivered under the Similitude of a Dream, Wherein is Discovered, The manner of his letting out, His Dangerous Journey; and safe Arrival at the Desired Countrey:*

> He had them into another room, where were a hen and chickens, and bid them observe a while. So one of the chickens went to the trough to drink; and every time she drank, she lifted up her head and her eyes toward heaven. "See," said he,

"what this little chick doth; and learn of her to acknowledge whence your mercies come, by receiving them with looking up. Yet again," said he, "observe and look." So they have heed, and perceived that the hen did walk in a fourfold method towards her chickens: 1. She had a common call, and that she hath all day long. 2. She had a special call, and that she had but sometimes. 3. She had a brooding note. (Matt. xxiii. 37.) And, 4. she had an outcry.

INTERPRETER: "Now," said he, "compare this hen to your King, and these chickens to His obedient ones: for, answerable to her, He Himself hath His methods which He walketh in towards His people. By His common call, He gives nothing; by His special call, He always has something to give; He also has a brooding voice, for them that are under His wing; and He hath an outcry, to give the alarm when He seeth the enemy come. I chose, my darlings, to lead you into the room where such things are, because you are women, and they are easy for you."

There are many apocryphal stories of soldiers on the battlefield being saved from a stray bullet by Bibles worn in their jacket pockets. But a reasonably documented case of a book being wielded in an attempt to ward off death occurred in 755: St. Boniface, the Anglo-Saxon missionary to Germany, used a book to defend himself from a pagan murderer's sword. Unsuccessfully. The book, mutilated with slashes from the blade, can still be seen in Fulda, Germany.

A more modern example of the utility of a bound volume as a kind of shield: Bob Emslie, a Canadian curveball pitcher in the late 1800s who became an umpire in baseball's major leagues, used to borrow hotel registers and wear them beneath his shirt as a chest protector.

And amateur hockey players across Canada – kids playing on frozen ponds and snow-strewn streets – used to make shin pads from the fat catalogues of the T. Eaton Co. department store chain, which were first issued as a 32-page booklet in 1884 and eventually grew to 900 pages before ceasing publication in 1976.

Emily Post, the Baltimore-born authority on social behavior, was the first popular adjudicator of good manners in North America. She published her original book on the subject in 1922 as *Etiquette in Society, in Business, in Politics and at Home*. Before her death in 1960 it had gone through 10 editions and 90 printings. She also wrote *How to Behave Though a Debutante* (1928). A later competitor in the etiquette industry was Amy Vanderbilt, whose *Complete Book of Etiquette* in 1958 contained this advice, which may or may not be dated, depending on your outlook:

- The remarriage of divorced people is always quiet, with only a few witnesses. Underage children are not permitted to attend.

- A thoughtful man, even if he is a nonsmoker, carries a lighter or matches so he can light a woman's cigarette.

- Men who are outdoors do not remove their hats unless a lady is present.

- Do not use first names unless invited to do so.

The concept of books as mere furnishings, rather than things to read, is nothing new. Seneca, the first-century Roman philosopher, delighted at the burning of the great Alexandria library: "Our idle book-hunters know about nothing but titles and bindings; their chests of cedar and ivory, and the book-cases that fill the bath-room, are nothing but fashionable furniture." A few bibliomaniacs have actually used books as furniture: Antonio Magliabecchi (1633-1714), librarian to the Grand Duke of Tuscany, could tolerate nothing but books around him, having only two chairs in his home, which he put together to form a bed. Often, though, he would throw a rug over a mound of books and sleep on them instead.

In *Crome Yellow* Aldous Huxley describes Mr. Bodiham's rectory study with its brown varnished bookshelves lined with thick theological works "which the second-hand booksellers generally sell by weight." In fact, not long after he wrote that, the 1927 catalogue of an Oxford book dealer offered "a quantity of well-bound Books, suitable as Furniture, at the following Clearance Prices. . . . Lists of Titles on application."

Books: These are great to fill empty wall units. Designers keep stacks of these in reserve for this purpose. Watch for sales sponsored by local libraries that need to clear stacks for new books. The covers of the books can relate to the color scheme of the room. Books also look nice stacked on a coffee table.

– *Florida Times-Union*, Jacksonville, Florida

93 · PERFUME

Charles Lamb, in *Essays of Elia* (1823), speaks of walking amid the foliage of books in an old library: "the odour of their old moth-scented coverings is fragrant as the first bloom of those sciential apples which grew amid the happy orchard." And Eugene Field writes, in *The Love Affairs of a Bibliomaniac*, that the man who opens the door of a bookcase "will be greeted by an outrush of odours that will prove to him beyond all doubt that books do actually consume air and exhale perfumes."

If the perfume of this or any book is not to your liking, you might follow the advice of John Power in *A Handy-Book about Books* (1870): "Musk, with one or two drops of oil of Neroli [an essential oil from the flowers of bitter orange], sponged on each side of the leaves and hung up to dry, will give a powerful odour. A more simple plan is, to place a vial of the mixture on the bookcase, or place there pieces of cotton impregnated with oil of cedar or birch."

Now for the bad news. The mere fact that you are reading this book may mean that you have more than a "normal" interest in books. *You may be* a bibliophile. Of course, you may be reading this to learn about the enemy. In which case, *you are* a bibliophobe.

Here for ready reference is a chart of book-related conditions and their symptoms:

Bibliobibulia: the reading of too many books.

Bibliokleptomania: the continual stealing of books.

Bibliolatry: the idolizing of books.

Bibliomania: the unrestrained collecting of books.

Bibliophagia: the eating of books, figuratively or literally (as by a bookworm).

Bibliophthoria: the destruction or ravaging of books, by a **biblioclast**.

Bibliotaphia: the burying, hiding, or hoarding of books.

William Ewart Gladstone, the 19th-century British prime minister
and author, was also a raving bibliomaniac. Once, asked by a bookstore owner which books he should send him, Gladstone flung his
arm out in an all-encompassing gesture and said, "Send me those!"
As the next customer found to his chagrin, the book collector had
bought every volume in the shop. But the statesman understood the
idea of books as a commodity, to be sold and resold: when too many
choked his library, he'd reluctantly sell them to secondhand booksellers. Well, he understood the concept to a point: very often the
dealers would resell him some of those same books, at a markup.

Book:

Anthology

Booklet

COMPILATION

Document

handbook

JOURNAL

Ledger

Libretto

MANUAL

MANUSCRIPT

Monograph

Novel

Novella

Opus

opuscule

Publication

SCREED

Script

TEXTBOOK

Thesis

Tome

TRACT

Treatise

VOLUME

Work

Some books pose the eternal questions; others attempt to furnish answers. Indeed, there are few books that do both.

> – The author of this book, who is not above concocting a quotation when an appropriate one is unavailable.

Here are the solutions to the puzzles posed in this book:

- Use No. 30. *Puzzle*: Alfred, Lord Tennyson, *Ulysses*:

    And tho'
    We are not now that strength which in old days
    Moved earth and heaven; that which we are, we are;
    One equal temper of heroic hearts,
    Made weak by time and fate, but strong in will
    To strive, to seek, to find and not to yield.

- Use No. 34. *Seducer*: 1-E, 2-F, 3-D, 4-A, 5-C, 6-B

- Use No. 75. *Riddle*: Each pair in the code refers to the number of a line in the riddle and the number of the word within that line. Deciphered, it spells out this answer: "He swallowed the paper and asked to see what the other paper in the chalice said." *Explanation*: Of course, the King was in front of all his subjects and could not admit in public that he had written *Death* on both pieces of paper.

A selective reference list of useful books about books:

Bader, Barbara. *American Picturebooks from* Noah's Ark *to* The Beast Within. New York: Macmillan, 1976.

Bettman, Otto L. *The Delights of Reading*. Boston: David R. Godine, 1987.

Birkerts, Sven. *The Gutenberg Elegies*. New York: Fawcett, 1995.

Burton, John Hill. *The Book-Hunter*. Edinburgh: William Blackwood and Sons, 1884.

Coysh, A. W. *Collecting Bookmarkers*. New York: Drake Publishers, 1974.

De Bury, Richard. *The Philobiblon*. Berkeley: University of California Press, 1948.

Donaldson, Gordon. *Books*. New York: Van Nostrand Reinhold, 1981.

Field, Eugene. *The Love Affairs of a Bibliomaniac*. London: John Lane, 1896.

Gold, Joseph. *Read for Your Life: Literature as a Life Support System*. Markham, ON: Fitzhenry and Whiteside, 1990.

Jackson, Holbrook. *The Anatomy of Bibliomania*. New York: Farrar, Straus, 1950.

Keddie, William. *Anecdotes Literary and Scientific*. London: James Blackwood, 1894.

Levarie, Norma. *The Art and History of Books*. New Castle, DE: Oak Knoll Press, 1995.

Lowery, Lawrence F. *Lowery's The Collector's Guide to Big Little Books and Similar Books*. Danville, CA: Educational Research and Applications Corp., 1981.

Olmert, Michael. *The Smithsonian Book of Books*. Washington, DC: Smithsonian Books, 1992.

Parsons, Nicholas. *The Book of Literary Lists*. London: Sidgwick and Jackson, 1985.

Pennac, Daniel. *Better Than Life*. Toronto: Coach House Press, 1994.

Power, John. *A Handy-Book about Books*. London: John Wilson, 1870.

Prance, Claude A. *Peppercorn Papers: A Miscellany on Books and Book-Collectors*. Cambridge: Golden Head Press, 1964.

Quayle, Eric. *The Collector's Book of Books*. London: Studio Vista, 1971.

Raabe, Tom. *Bibliohilism: The Literary Addiction*. Golden, CO: Fulcrum Publishing, 1991.

Targ, William, ed. *Carousel for Bibliophiles*. Metuchen, NJ: Scarecrow Reprint, 1967.

Taylor, Alan, ed. *Long Overdue: A Library Reader*. London: Library Association Publishing and Mainstream Publishing, 1993.

Tebbel, John. *Between Covers: The Rise and Transformation of American Book Publishing*. New York: Oxford University Press, 1987.

The most utilitarian index for book-lovers might very well be the Roman Catholic Church's *Index Librorum Prohibitorum*, which Pope Paul IV launched in 1559 as a list of books that Catholics were forbidden to read because of their heretical or profane content. Until it was abandoned in 1966, the Index numbered more than 4,000 titles, including some of the most influential and well-written works of all time. Among them:

Abelard, Pierre, all works (heresy), 1559.

Balzac, Honoré de, all works (immorality), 1841.

Calvin, John, all works (heresy), 1559.

Casanova, Giovanni, *Mémoires* (immorality), 1834.

Cervantes, Miguel de, *Don Quixote* (impiety), 1676.

Descartes, René, a selection of philosophical works (heresy), 1633; *Meditations* and six other works (heresy), 1948.

Diderot, Denis, *L'Encyclopédie,* seven volumes (irreligiosity), 1752.

Dumas, Alexandre, all romantic stories (immorality), 1863.

Erasmus, *Opera Omnia* (heresy), 1559.

Flaubert, Gustave, *Salammbö* and *Madame Bovary* (immorality), 1864.

France, Anatole, all works (immorality), 1922.

Gibbon, Edward, *The Decline and Fall of the Roman Empire* (subversiveness), 1783.

Gide, André, all works (immorality, etc.), 1952.

Hugo, Victor, *Notre Dame de Paris* and *Les Misérables* (immorality), 1834.

La Fontaine, Jean, *Contes Nouvelles en Vers* (impiety, etc.), 1703.

Locke, John, *An Essay Concerning Human Understanding* (impiety), 1700.

Maeterlinck, Maurice, all works (immorality and irreligiosity), 1914.

Montaigne, Michel, *Les Essaies* (impiety), 1676.

Richardson, Samuel, *Pamela* (immorality), 1755.

Rousseau, Jean-Jacques, *Lettres de la Montagne* and *Emile* (immorality and irreligiosity), 1763.

Sade, Marquis de, *Justine* and *Juliette* (obscenity), 1791.

Sartre, Jean-Paul, all works (subversiveness), 1948.

Sterne, Laurence, *A Sentimental Journey* (immorality), 1819.

Swift, Jonathan, *A Tale of a Tub* (impiety and subversiveness), 1734.

Voltaire, François, *Lettres Philosophiques* (immorality), 1752.

Endpaper (noun): Blank leaf at beginning or end of a book.

ABOUT THE AUTHOR

PAUL GRESCOE has written for major magazines such as
Maclean's, TV Guide, and *Reader's Digest* and is the author of two
mystery novels, *Flesh Wound* (winner of the Crime Writers of
Canada Best First Novel Award) and *Blood Vessel.* With his wife,
Audrey, he has also written *Fragments of Paradise: British
Columbia's Wild and Wondrous Islands* and *Alaska: The Cruise-
Lover's Guide.* Paul and Audrey Grescoe live on Bowen Island,
British Columbia.

ABOUT THE ILLUSTRATOR

BRUCE ROBERTS is an award-winning illustrator whose work
has appeared in the *Washington Post* and on ABC-TV. Roberts lives
with his wife and daughter in Montreal.